MW01296678

Once A Nun

Esmé Frances Moreira

A beautiful young woman became a Franciscan Nun

Real life accounts of events in an English religious order in the fifties and sixties.

Once A Nun by Esmé Frances Moreira

Printed by CreateSpace, an Amazon.com

ISBN 9781729562857

1st Edition 2018

Available from Amazon.com

Once A Nun by Esmé Frances Moreira

Introduction

My decision to become a nun and later to leave the order were deeply considered and not taken lightly. There were many things I enjoyed about religious life however the hypocrisy I witnessed led me to want to be free again.

I continue to live a deeply spiritual life with a direct connection to Him, although I no longer feel the need to attend Mass on a regular basis.

These stories are my own, from my recollections with some help from friends who were there also.

Dedication

This book is dedicated to my friends
in the convents around the world.
I believe in your work and prayers and
your dedication to the three Vows of Poverty
Obedience and Chastity.

Index

'We led our lives accordingly, conscious of how much Saint Francis of Assisi loved his Lady Poverty, as he called her and lived by her standards'

Praying in Ladywell Chapel 1960's

Forward

I have known and loved Esmé since the first time we spoke by telephone after meeting on an internet dating site in 2005.

I have heard her stories; I have watched her tell them to others. I have listened to her tell people about this book.

Once A Nun is about a spirited, intelligent woman who mistook a calling to religious life for an opportunity to repair her parent's marriage damaged due to being separated during World War Two.

Esmé's life is about community, family, friendship, and laughter. It is also about questioning vows and practices that do nothing to strengthen faith, but break down character.

Esmé with her golden aura and healing hands is the only person I have met who unequivocally charms all who meet her, and she is adored by all who take the time to get to know her.

I give you Esmé's *Once A Nun.*

Julie Apostolu

Esmé at 1 year
Batu Gajah, Perak,
Malaya

Esmé 9, mother & sister
In Bangalore, India

Esmé 14, with her sister
Ipoh, Malaysia, post war

From Esmé's Photograph Album

1

Before I Became a Nun

I never expected to become a nun. My education was with various groups of nuns in Malaysia, India, and Australia. I did not particularly like nuns or religion, so to actually decide to become one was not in my mind. I valued their work in the education of children in those countries and the other types of work such as running nursing homes and hospitals.

My primary schooling which was before the start of World War Two was at Convent Schools run by the Dames de Saint Maur in Ipoh, and Taiping, cities in Malaysia. During the war, 1942 and 1945, my secondary schooling was in Bangalore, India. One school was run by the Good Shepherd Sisters and the other by the Sisters of Saint Joseph.

After the Second World War I returned to Ipoh Convent School with the Dames de Saint Maur for three years, and then my parents sent me to 'finishing school' at Santa Maria College, Attadale, a southern suburb of Perth, Western Australia.

Santa Maria College was an elite boarding and day school for girls situated on the banks of the Swan River from where we could look back across this serpentine river toward the city of Perth; a beautiful sight, particularly at night as we sat studying. The Sisters of Mercy are an extensive institution of the Catholic Church and we had a sister school in Perth City called the Victoria Square Ladies College now called Mercedes College.

The nuns were mostly kind to us but discipline was a high determinant as to one's progress. I found their enlightened outlook refreshing but that did not stop me from giving each of them a nickname; Sister Philomena was Flop, Sister Stephanie was Steph, and Sister Margaret Mary Alacoque was Aggie Whopper. The Principal of the school, who also taught the senior girls was Sister Bertrand known by me as Bert. The Mother Superior of the school community was Sister Dolores or Dolly. Of course my friends knew my mischievous nicknames for our teachers.

Midnight feasts were helped along by our day-girl friends who purchased the food for us, and then it was smuggled into a hiding place. Whether the nuns knew we never found out. Once when I was ill with the flu Mother Dolores visited me. The food for our midnight feed had been stowed under my bed in preparation for our scheduled night's feast. I was sure Mother could smell the oranges, but she didn't utter a word. What a champion she was!

As a young child I had learned to play the piano at my aunt's and later I had formal piano lessons. I remember and appreciate the comprehensive training we received from our music teacher, Sister Eunan at Santa Maria College. A nun of many years she was highly qualified in music and choral singing; equivalent to a professor. Her regular choral work with the choir

2

improved the quality of what we sang, and the lessons we learned from her remained with us. During the three years I spent at Santa Maria our school entered the West Australian Eisteddfod Competition which we won each year for three consecutive years and the choir was asked to sing on the Perth radio.

I was free from nuns when I left school at age eighteen. I spent one sociable year in Perth, attending university and trying various positions to determine where my interests lay. Back home in Ipoh Malaysia again I sat looking out to the garden at my parent's home, thinking. I should make serious plans for my future; I needed to decide on a career. I was nearly twenty one and I didn't know what I was going to do with my life. I was aware that my father would be delighted if I became a medical doctor like him, but I leaned towards Physiotherapy.

World War Two had had a negative effect on my parent's marriage. My father had remained in Malaysia and my mother, sister and I were evacuated to India. Four years was a long time to be apart. The negative effect of the separation concerned me, and I wished I could repair the damage that the time apart had had on my parent's lives. Maybe, if I serve God then He would look favorably on my parent's marriage, and they would become united, and once again their marriage will be happy.

Chirping birds, a gentle breeze wafting through the open windows and above all the peace and serenity helped the thinking process. That peace was broken by the ring of the telephone. I recognized the familiar voice.
'Hi, may I speak to Esmé please?'
'Hello, Siew Ming'.
'Glad I got you, I thought you might be interested to hear that I have just met some nuns who are quite

3

different to what we are used to. They are dressed in white, drive their own car and are looking for girls to see a film they are showing about their life and work. Would you be interested in seeing this film, Esmé?'

'Sounds interesting, there is nothing much happening here. Would you like me to pick you up?' As I set the phone back in its cradle, I wondered if this could be a pathway for my life.

The day came and I picked up Siew Ming at the appointed time and we drove to the Ipoh Convent. At the front entrance Sister Jeanne Marie sat on guard and she told us the number of the classroom. We were met by a tall nun dressed in full white regalia. She welcomed us in crisp English tones and introduced herself as Sister Mary Campion.

'Please sit and we will start shortly.' Another Sister approached us.

'I am Sister Rosaria, and it is nice to meet you.' She spoke with an Irish brogue. The room filled rapidly and soon there were about twenty young women apparently eager to see the movie.

Sister Campion welcomed us. She told us that they belonged to a group of Roman Catholic nuns called the Franciscan Missionaries of the Divine Motherhood, known as FMDMs based in Surrey England. They had recently arrived in Singapore at the request of the Bishop of Singapore and Malaysia. The Sisters had been doing missionary work in China and were no longer needed there.

By showing the movies in various towns in Malaysia and in Singapore, they hoped to attract young women to dedicate their lives to God. These nuns serve God through various types of work including nursing and midwifery, as well as the other medical and administrative disciplines found in hospitals. Teachers and future teachers were also welcome. Interested

4

young women would 'enter' in Singapore for a couple of months and then transfer to England. They would experience two and a half years of religious training, after which they would be sent to train in their chosen fields. If they chose a medical training they could later work in the hospitals being built in Singapore and Malaysia.

'Now, Sister Rosaria, will show the films of the life of our community and the religious training through the various stages.'

Sister Rosaria started the first of several short films and we saw a line of young nuns processing through monastic-like corridors. The women wore bridal dresses with veils typical of their culture. These were Postulants, who after six months living in the convent were by wearing their bridal dresses signifying they were 'Brides of Christ'.

The Mother General, assisted by the Novice Mistress, stood on the altar steps helping slip the white habit and the parts of the habit over the bridal dresses. Each bride recited her Vows to indicate her serious intention to live her life governed by the principles of Poverty, Chastity, and Obedience.

Following the brides were a number of nuns dressed in white habits, with white veils. These were Novices who after two years of study would commit by taking their First Vows or make their First Profession. Symbolic of this occasion they received a sky blue veil which is worn over their white veil when entering into a Holy place for worship.

The movie showed the group processing out of the Chapel to a reception with their families and friends.

Another film showed Novice Sisters dressed in white habits with 'Blue Aprons' as they were also called, after a few months living as a nun, doing a multitude of chores, cleaning of the many buildings of the Convent, servicing machines in various areas and sewing and tailoring in the sewing area. It depicted them cooking for the community and managing the farm. The Novices were feeding and caring for the animals, using tractors, ploughing fields and harvesting crops, replacing tiles on roofs and performing up-keep to the buildings. The nuns ran their own printing press, producing documents and newsletters, posters and flyers when required. It certainly was not what I expected of convent life.

At home that evening I wrote a letter to Sister Campion asking more questions about the Sisters and their Franciscan lives. Having heard during my schooling about Saint Francis of Assisi and his concept for the lives of his Franciscan Friars and religious Sisters, I found their idea of Lady Poverty as they called her, intriguing. Saint Francis had come from a wealthy family background and preferred a life of poverty to serve His Lord.

Our family lived a comfortable lifestyle but I had noticed that my parents weren't the same happy people they had been prior to the war. After weeks of deep thinking I reasoned, in my naivety, that if I offered or sacrificed my life to the service of God the marriage could be improved. I believed I was called in order to make my parent's lives happier.

2

Becoming a Postulant

The hot muggy night did nothing to help me sleep as I pondered on how to break the news to my parents on my decision to 'enter' the religious life. I knew my mother would be proud though sad to lose me, but my father was a different proposition. He had high hopes that at twenty years of age, I would follow his lead and choose medicine as a career. I could share that these Franciscan nuns I was planning to join, ran hospitals and nursing homes that included maternity, medical and surgical wards, homes for unmarried mothers, and orphanages for children. My father would then see how medical skills of varying sorts would be used in those circumstances.

Next morning at breakfast I announced, 'I've decided I would like to become a Franciscan Missionary of the Divine Motherhood.' Silence. You could hear a pin drop. My twelve year old sister said, 'You want to become a nun? Won't you be locked away behind closed walls?'
'In a way I will, but when I met these nuns and they told me of the work they do, I thought how wonderful it would be to work in the medical field with a choice to be a doctor, nurse, midwife, physiotherapist,

pharmacist, haematologist or any career needed to run hospitals and nursing homes. They drive cars and ambulances, and spend their lives in service to people in all walks of life.'

'I had no idea,' said my father. 'So it may still be possible that you could choose medicine as a career?'

'Maybe Dad, it will be a choice between medicine and physiotherapy; I would enjoy both. However as nuns, they spend the first two and a half years training in the life of a religious. If they are thought ready to take First Vows after the training period, they then can train at whatever career they or their superiors choose.'

'That's interesting,' said my mother. 'You actually get a choice, that's unusual for nuns.'

Breaking my news to the family proved to be not as difficult as I had thought. I could see that my father was thoughtful but hopeful, my mother proud to have a daughter a nun, and my only sister curious and interested. One big hurdle was over.

A list was sent to me of the items I would need: clothing, my records of birth, baptism, and education. My mother and I went shopping for the clothing and the time flew by.

The day for my arrival was agreed with Reverend Mother; Wednesday, 6 January 1954, Feast of the Epiphany. I would 'enter' the Convent arriving straight from Singapore airport. My hometown of Ipoh was four hundred and fifty miles north of Singapore the island lying at the base of the Malay Peninsula. The Franciscan Missionaries of the Divine Motherhood had no convents in Malaysia, but worked at a large hospital called Tan Tock Seng Hospital in Singapore. The Sisters lived next door to the hospital in a large two storied house within the hospital grounds. Plans were afoot to build a hospital in Singapore that would be run by the Franciscan Missionaries of the Divine Motherhood.

8

My father insisted on accompanying me on the two hour flight to Singapore. When we arrived at the Convent we met the Reverend Mother and Sisters dressed in their white robes, chatted to them and then my father turned to me to say farewell. The nuns left us alone and I assured him that I would do my best at whatever lay before me, that I would miss him and the family, but that I felt compelled to make a life of my own. Tearfully, we hugged and said our goodbyes, and he walked to the door where the taxi awaited him.

The Sisters made me welcome as Reverend Mother introduced me. We sat down to the evening meal, followed by an hour's recreation before retiring for the night.

I learned that FMDM's, despite taking three simple Vows, value the Vow of Poverty over Obedience and Chastity. We led our lives accordingly; conscious of how much Saint Francis of Assisi loved his 'Lady Poverty' as he called her, and lived by her standards.

As I walked through the rooms of the house I observed that the furniture was simple but comfortable. Like houses in Malaysia, there was a separate block of rooms behind the house, which included a kitchen, bed-rooms and a bathroom for domestic help. I was introduced to the Chinese woman who lived there; she cooked meals for the Sisters, and I met the woman who came in to clean the house and do the laundry and ironing.

Except for Sister Mary Baptista who had been assigned to guide me for the next two months, the other Sisters including Reverend Mother worked every day at the hospital performing nursing and midwifery duties required of them.

The Sisters wore long white habits adding a white apron during their nursing duties. My Postulant's dress was a short white dress, a small white veil covering my head, a cape to wear if necessary, white socks, and shoes.

The morning after my arrival I was allowed to sleep in until just before 7.00 am when I was woken in time for the early morning Mass. At my initiation that day, I was informed that the morning call for me was at 5.00 am from then on, for the chanting of the Divine Office; as all monks, priests and nuns do every day. Contrary to popular belief Catholic nuns are directly under the Pope as far as religious laws and practices are concerned, and are subject to the local bishop for the work they do in the area of his jurisdiction.

A French priest arrived to say Mass each morning and he was served breakfast following the Mass. I later heard that one of the Sisters waited on him and often Reverend Mother chatted to him as he dined.

After breakfast, Sister Baptista took me into a separate room where I received my first instructions on my life as a Postulant and as a resident of the Convent. On this morning, she read out the Rules I was expected to practise, which to me sounded like a long list of Do Not's. When she finished, she asked, 'So, have you questions or anything to say about these Rules, Esmé?'

Reflecting for a moment, I answered, 'It looks like I can't do anything without asking permission, even to drink a glass of water, except possibly breathe, and that's involuntary anyway!'

Sister Baptista's tall spare frame shook as she laughed. 'Yes, I can see that seems true, but remember this period is training for religious life. It's hard to begin with, but it will get easier as you go along. Don't ever

10

forget that God never tries you without giving you the strength to cope. Accept what you're asked to do with willingness and joy, and God will give you the grace to be at peace.

'FMDMs have a period of training of six months as a Postulant, which you are at now. The next stage, if you are deemed to be ready, is two years as a Novice. During the first year, called the Canonical year, you do not encounter people outside of the convent or hospital. In the second year of your Noviciate, you are given assignments which permit you to meet the people we serve; like patients in hospital for instance, but conversation with them is limited to brief greetings and necessities.

'The strict Rules of Silence limit us to use the minimum conversation during our work hours and only on necessary actions. At recreation twice a day, once in the afternoon and once at night, we have time when we can converse freely with our Sisters and relax. However there are limitations to those conversations too. We do not talk about our past, or family, so the dialogue is about the daily events or work in our lives. Do you think you can do that Esmé?'

I thought for a moment. 'Silence has never been easy for me Sister, but I can see that I will have to try my best. I think this is going to be an interesting adventure, and I am a born adventurer. I love challenges in life, they make me rise to the occasion. People are important to me, and my life has always been filled with friends. This is going to be a personal challenge, which I hope by the grace of God I can do.'
Sister smiled. 'If you ever have difficulties with the rules, come and talk to me about it. Remember my door is open to you.'

11

'Thank you, Sister. I assure you I will come to see you when I've made great efforts to keep the Daily Rule as best I can.'
'I'm sure you will, and that too is part of your training; not allowing too much independence so that you're free to live a life of humility and Obedience.'

She showed me the Library where I could choose a book I wanted to read. I chose *No Man Is An Island* by the American Cistercian Monk named Thomas Merton. I treasured reading this deeply spiritual book; it took over a year to complete it.

She advised me that a bell would ring to announce the midday meal and that I should make my way to the dining room to join the other Sisters. During daily meals one of the Sisters would read from a spiritual book as the nuns ate in silence. The Sisters who worked at the hospital returned for the midday meal. This was followed by a short siesta in our own rooms. I was grateful for a chance for a nap after getting up so early each day. An hour for recreation in the community room followed, after which the Sisters returned to work at the hospital.

Sister Baptista advised me that we would meet again in the same room after the afternoon recreation for the next activity on the Training Calendar. There would be another short period of instruction before the evening meal when the Sisters returned from the hospital. This would be followed by the evening prayer and the night recreation.

Sister explained to me that the program for the day was called the Daily Horarium and that if I forgot what came next, to refer to the list on the wall. At first I needed to check the Horarium to remind myself of things, but before long I knew the program.

Sister told me to go to the Chapel to complete my personal prayers for the day. This meant half an hour of meditation, half an hour of spiritual reading, followed by completions of the Catholic ritual of the Stations of the Cross.

Esmé aged 19, 1952
From Esmé's Photograph Album

3

My Journey to England

It was on Saturday, 6 March 1954, exactly two months since I 'entered' the Franciscan Missionaries of the Divine Motherhood, that I flew from Singapore to London on my first long air journey of my life.

Awoken by the sound of *Laudate Jesus Christus,* Praise Jesus Christ, uttered repeatedly in Latin by the Sister-in-Charge of waking the community, I got out of bed hurriedly going through the morning ablutions and dressed in my Postulant's garb of the simple dress and black cape and made my way to the Chapel for Morning Prayer. Today I wore a black dress; an indication to the community that I was leaving the tropics and going to cooler climes. My mind was distracted with the imminent flight and arrival in England. Exciting as one's first ever long flight is, there was also an element of nervousness niggling in the background.

Breakfast, normally in silence, buzzed today with the sounds of Sisters wishing me a happy time in England during the six years of training in religious life. The Rule of Silence was dispensed with during that morning by the Mother Superior so the Sisters could

15

bid me bon voyage. Many of the Sisters asked me to pass on messages to various Sisters in England. What struck me was their friendliness and obvious sincerity to myself and to their Sisters in Christ in England.

I returned to my room, picked up my packed suitcase and made my way downstairs to the foyer where Mother Angela and Sister Baptista waited.
'Here is your passport and tickets Sister, which you will need to keep handy and in a safe place. Now say goodbye to the Sisters, and we will be on our way to the airport.'

I hugged and said goodbye to each Sister. The whole community waved goodbye and I waved from the back seat. That sight of twelve white clad Sisters in their habits and veils, waving with smiles on their faces, is a picture that has remained with me.

The journey across Singapore Island from the city area to the airport was brisk. In the sweltering equatorial heat, waves of heat rose up from the asphalted roads to hit us as we drove along. At the airport, Mother Angela parked the car and the nuns accompanied me to the check-in counter. Once my suitcase had been checked, they said their goodbyes and watched me walk into the restricted area to go through the formalities of Customs and Immigration. With a final wave, I made my way into the transit area.

As I waited to board the flight to London Heathrow, I could not help wondering where my seat was and who would be sitting beside me. I found my seat number and put my hand luggage into the over head locker. A kindly looking sari-clad Indian woman sat next to the window which meant my seat was on the aisle. I was relieved, as this meant I would not need to climb over other passengers to visit the toilet.

As I seated myself, I smiled at the Indian lady. 'Hello, my name is Madhuri, and yours is?'

'My name is Esmé and I am flying to London. What about you?'

'I am flying to London too, and I hope we can enjoy the flight together.'

After we had settled into our seats, she continued, 'I'm flying to London to attend a Conference for Dermatologists. Every so often we need to update our knowledge to keep up with developments around the world.'

We fastened our seat belts, and the flight attendants proceeded to run through the safety drill. The engines started and the plane moved slowly forward to taxi down the runway prior to take-off. The throb of the engine increased my excitement. Before I realised it, we found ourselves airborne and looking down on the vast Kallang Airport of Singapore from British Airways Flight 751.

An hour after we took off, we were served a meal; and we settled into our seats to have a nap. Our first stop was Dubai; seven hours from take-off at Singapore. Neither of us wished to disembark as we knew how hot it would be, so we stayed aboard and chatted. The forty-five minute stop was soon over and we departed for Amsterdam, four hours away. We decided we would walk around the airport there, and have a light meal. After the wholesome meals at the convent, the airplane fare left a lot to be desired.

At Amsterdam we arrived at an area with shops. Shopping for me was not allowed as I was a Franciscan who lived the Vow of Poverty. Before long I would take Vows and earthly acquisitions were unnecessary in my life.

Two kind gentlemen from our flight followed us around and were there in case we had problems with the language or dealings in the shops. Then we made our way to the café. Presently we were enjoying coffee and delicious sandwiches, cakes, buns and Dutch delicacies. I was grateful for the kindness of my companions who paid for the coffee and cakes; I didn't carry money and had none given to me for the trip. Listening to the chatter I realized that I missed this interchange of opinion and easy conversation. I also realised in my new life as a nun it would not be correct to join in the conversation so I kept quiet and just listened. Not an easy thing for me to do!

Once aboard again we settled into our seats and we were up in the air. The Captain advised that the flight to London Heathrow took two hours and that today the weather in London was fine and sunny. Thank God for that, I said to myself, as I didn't want any bumps or dramas as we landed.

Before I could close my eyes, the Captain announced over the intercom that we were shortly to arrive in London and would be circling the airport. We landed smoothly, disembarked and with Immigration and Customs completed I wheeled my trolley out to the arrivals area. I spotted two penguin-like figures waving from the far corner. They wore floor length black cloaks over their habits; quite a different look to the white clad Sisters in the tropics, who didn't require long cloaks to keep warm. They said tentatively 'Esmé?' in unison. How anyone could fail to see who I was, dressed as I was!

They greeted me and shook hands with decorum. As we walked I learned that they had travelled for an hour to Heathrow to meet me. Mother Bernadette was Irish, lively and gregarious; a vibrant personality. Sister Redemptor had a French accent but spoke English fluently. Later I learned she was Belgian. She was the quieter of the two. We headed to Surrey where the Motherhouse of the Franciscan Missionaries of the Divine Motherhood and the Nursing Home were situated.

I was pleased to be back on terra firma again as I was not a particularly good traveller. At that stage of my life I had lived in Malaysia, Singapore, India, and Australia and appreciated the different customs and cultures; however not the traveling to and from each place, as I always felt very nauseated.

So, here I was, twenty years of age, over six thousand miles away from my homeland Singapore and Malaysia, and I was about to start my religious life.

Ladywell Chapel, Godalming, Surrey

The new Chapel built at the Motherhouse in Godalming was officially opened in 1962. It is a beautiful Chapel with a semicircular wall of mosaics behind the main altar. High in the centre on the mosaic dome behind the altar is a Franciscan crucifix painted on the wall and below is the Virgin Mary holding baby Jesus. On either side are paintings of the prominent Franciscans; Saint Francis of course, and Saint Clare who was the first Franciscan woman to follow Francis, along with other Catholic saints.

Ladywell Convent was purchased by FMDM's in 1956.
The new Chapel at Ladywell was opened in 1962.
View Ladywell Convent films on YouTube:
- *Nun's Vows at Ladywell Convent (1962)*
- *Farming Nuns (1967)*
- *Nuns at Work (1965).*

www.ladywellretreat.org.uk/home/
This property is now used as a FMDM Retreat and Spiritual Centre.

http://fmdminternational.co.uk/our-fmdm-family

4

My First English Winter

On an extremely cold autumn morning I walked the half mile up the hill from the Noviciate House called Portiuncula, to the Mount Alvernia Nursing Home in Guildford where our Community Chapel was situated.

In the foyer outside the Chapel entrance was a tall black chest of drawers where the nuns kept their veils and prayer books. Professed Sisters who had been in training for two years wore sky blue veils over their daily white veil and Novices wore white veils over their daily white veil when entering a place of worship.

The Great Silence prevailed as the Sisters gathered in the foyer hurriedly donning veils and collecting their Breviaries containing the Psalms before entering the Chapel.

Now in England my mornings started half an hour earlier. I rose at 4.30 am for two and a half hours of prayers, meditation and chanting of the Divine Office. Following this the Sisters remained in the Chapel for the celebration of Mass by a priest.

Born just five degrees north of the Equator in Malaysia, I was used to tropical weather, so never before had I seen snow or experienced the cold of an English winter. The cold was noticeable because wherever Sisters gathered as a community there was no heating because of our Vow of Poverty. In time I learned that when snow was expected, the temperature zoomed down to low levels and once the snow had fallen, the temperatures warmed up; slightly!

Beginning with short morning prayers and reciting the seven decades of our Franciscan rosary, we then entered the silent phase for half an hour of meditation. When this ended, we stood ready to commence chanting Matins of the Divine Office.

The Chapel was rectangular in shape and along the long walls and facing each other were sets of carved wooden stalls with kneelers. The hinged seats folded back allowing the Sisters to kneel facing the altar in their own stalls. At the opposite end from the altar were three stalls positioned centrally for the Superior and two visiting senior Sisters. Aligned with the three stalls was the organ and stool for the organist who was one of the nuns.

The windows above the seats were stained glass. The altar stood at the top of the rectangle with a door for the priest to enter from the corridor.

The Chapel was darkened with the only light visible being the flickering of the oil tabernacle light which was never extinguished. Silence reigned; as the Sisters having finished the vocal prayers now knelt or sat meditating in silence.

As I knelt trying to meditate I felt colder with every passing minute. My head spun, I felt I was going to be sick because I was so cold. I started to shiver. The woollen cardigan we were permitted to wear under our habits proved woefully inadequate to keep me warm. Unable to stand it another minute, I arose and walked down the center aisle to where Reverend Mother was praying. I whispered that I needed to leave the Chapel and she nodded her approval.

As I passed the dresser in the foyer, I flung off my white Novice veil and hurried down the corridor in the direction of a toilet. I remember passing the priest's entry to the Chapel and then everything went black.

Sometime later, I heard the voice of Reverend Mother Bernadette saying loudly, 'Sit up, Sister!' From the depths of unconsciousness I sat bolt upright, in a dazed fashion. Mother helped me up and took me down the corridor, down some steps to an empty patient's room where she sat me in a comfortable armchair in front of a wall heater.
'Stay there and do not move. Father will bring you Communion, and a Sister will bring you breakfast later. Today you will stay here and keep warm and we will notify Sister that you will not be attending to your duties today.'

It was the cold that had this effect on me. I later heard that the Night Sister was walking to a patient's room to wake her, when she saw a still form on the floor outside the Priest's entry to the Chapel. She immediately rushed to my side and softly called my name. There was no response. She could not see if I was breathing. Being from Asia, she believed it was bad luck to walk past a dead body, so she rushed back to the steps leading down to her maternity floor, along the corridor leading to the medical wards and back up a long flight of stairs and to the Chapel where she reported to Reverend Mother in the Chapel, that I was DEAD!

23

Reverend Mother hurried out to where I lay on the floor and said those memorable words 'Sit up, Sister!' to which I immediately responded, though in a dazed fashion. Just like Christ I thought. But in this instance; 'She is risen!' I wanted to ask Reverend Mother, 'Did you feel like Christ raising the dead?' but it was our Great Silence, so I remained quiet.

* * * * *

English winters are not just cold they are damp and this damp went right through my bones. Winter is another time when allergies are rife. I happened to be an unhappy target, and that first winter found me with a streaming nose from early in the morning and until midday each day, every day.

One of the rules which I had difficulty obeying was when we were chanting the Divine Office we were not permitted to put down our breviaries, until the Office was completed. I found that with a streaming nose it proved impossible to blow my nose without using two hands to hold the handkerchief. This necessitated putting the breviary down, digging my handkerchief out of the deep habit pocket, unfolding the man-sized handkerchief and blowing down the fold, repeatedly, then refolding the handkerchief and putting it back in my pocket. I then picked up the breviary and tried to find the place where everyone was at. Initially I was unaware that my series of actions were being followed by a few of the Sisters who giggled at this repetitive breaking of the rule; a rule which seemed to have no real purpose.

Later I discovered that the English and Irish Sisters noticed that Singaporean and Malayan Sisters folded

24

our handkerchiefs neatly, and when it was necessary to use them, we opened them out, blew down a central line and refold the handkerchief; unlike our English Sisters who bundled their hankies into their pockets higgle-de-piggle-dee. The handkerchief was supposed to last a whole week. Now for those of us with allergies and streaming noses, how could we keep to this ridiculous rule? With a nose that streamed from the time I woke until midday, the handkerchief was absolutely soaked in no time at all. Strangely I was never corrected or upbraided for breaking the rule, and life went on.

Ladywell Convent, Godalming, Surrey

Sister Regina Mundi, after First Vows 1956
From Esmé's Photograph Album

5

Progress to Novice

Weeks before our group was to be made Novices; I was called into Mother Francis' office.

'Sister you are considered suitable to become a Novice. Is there a particular name you would choose for your life as a religious Sister?'

'The two I can think of are Monica or Veronica, Mother,' I replied.

'Unfortunately those names are taken, and the Sisters are still living. I have thought about it and this year is the celebration of Mary as Queen of the World which in Latin is Regina Mundi. Do you like that?'

I nodded my head. 'That sounds like a nice name.'

'Good Sister, and that's what you will be, Sister Regina Mundi.'

I had trained for six months as a Postulant, and now I was deemed suitable to train for two years as a Novice. To celebrate this progress a ceremony would take place with the Postulants dressed as brides. This is known as our Wedding Day or Clothing Ceremony. The wedding dresses were supplied by families for the occasion; my mother had a wedding gown made in Malaysia and posted it to me for the occasion. As none of my family in Malaysia was able to attend, I valued my dress as a symbol of family support for my progress. It made my dress special to me.

Postulants were permitted to wear their ethnic costumes they would have worn had they been married in their own countries. This made the ceremony colorful. Of course we wore white stockings and shoes so there were no heels marking the wooden parquet floors.

For the ceremony in the Chapel, we processed in slowly to organ music and singing. The priest said prayers and when each bride in turn went up to the altar, he offered a prayer and then with scissors snipped a lock of hair from the front, back and each side of her head signifying that the woman about to take Vows was sacrificing her crowning glory to be a Bride of Christ.

Clothing, as donning of the habit was called came next. The Mother General pulled a white habit over my bridal gown, right there on the altar steps! I felt as though I was the size of a house with two sets of clothing on my body. First the habit, a loose cotton drill gown from neck to ankles with straight long sleeves to the wrists. Cinching in the waist was a Franciscan cord with three large white knots on one end which hung down the right side of the habit. These knots symbolized the three Vows of Poverty, Chastity and Obedience. On the left side a large brown seven decade rosary hung from the cord around the waist; as opposed to the usual five decade rosary.

In quick succession a length of the habit material with an opening in the middle was placed over my head; it hung front and back and was called the scapular. Next followed the guimpe; a shaped collar across the upper chest that covered my shoulders and came up the neck and over the ears to tie with tapes across the back of my head. Then the band, which spanned my forehead, was tied at the back with tapes. Lastly, the veil which had three stiffening boards inserted to frame the face was placed on my head. The veil fell to about mid body or the level of the elbows. We were given prayer books and bibles, and our religious names; Sister Regina Mundi was now my name, and on our heads we wore a Crown of Flowers to celebrate our commitment. Later we removed our bridal attire and changed into just the habit. From that time on the habit with all of its parts would be the clothes we would wear.

Novices as we were now called started two years of Noviciate. During this time we received our religious training from the Novice Mistress. Each year we renewed our Vows of Poverty, Chastity and Obedience and when we came to the Fifth Renewal if we were deemed suitable we were able to take our Final Vows at the completion of six years of training.

The next morning after Mass and breakfast we began the day with an hour's lecture; training in the life of a Novice. The Novice Mistress, Sister Andrew explained the reason for our Vows and for the things required of us in our daily lives. Examples of how this could be practised were given, and I haven't forgotten. Obedience was explained thus; when death occurs and before 'rigor mortis', the body is malleable and can be placed in any position easily. This was an example of perfect Obedience. Another example was given; if we are asked to plant a cabbage tree upside down, just do it, without question.

The one Vow of the Jesuits is Obedience because it covers all other Vows or rules. Everything comes under the umbrella of Obedience.

* * * * *

Franciscan Novices were assigned different tasks every twelve weeks during our two years of spiritual training. This ensured we learnt the work necessary to run our large private Mount Alvernia Nursing Home, Guilford. Novices usually performed the menial tasks around the hospital like cooking and scullery duties, cleaning of patient's rooms and waiting areas on each floor of the medical, surgical and maternity wings. The fully equipped laundry and the garden were attended by the Novices. During these two years I didn't meet outsiders, far less talk with them.

I was assigned cleaning and also to be in charge of the bell ringing for three months; the bell represented the 'Call of God' for the Sisters. At 12 noon and 6.00 pm the bell was rung for Sisters' and patients' meals.

On my first day, I was busy cleaning a patients' room, when I suddenly remembered that the bell needed to be rung. I looked at my pocket watch and was horrified to see I was ten minutes late. It was after midday and the patients received their midday meals on the dot of twelve.

I rushed to where the bell was housed; it rested on a thick mat in an alcove opposite the entrance to the Chapel. Seizing the six inch long wooden handle, I rang it as vigorously as I could. The heavy brass bell and the wooden handle, proved to be unwieldy to swing and ring, but I managed to do so, loudly and strongly.

Just as I returned the bell to its hallowed place, the Novice Mistress appeared from her room down the corridor.
'Sister, this is serious. When the bell is not rung at the correct time it disrupts our routine; the patients don't receive their meals on time; the nursing Sisters are out of 'sync'; the operating rooms are not ready; and the

whole day becomes topsy-turvy for everyone. For this transgression, you will wear the bell around your neck for every meal in the community refectory, for one week.' With that she turned on her heel and disappeared into her room.

It struck me that this was humiliating to say the least, especially as I knew that every time I took a mouthful, the bell would ring. Nevertheless, it was my fault and I had to accept the appropriate punishment without question. Well, I said to myself; best get on with it!

I looked in the drawers below the bell housing, and found a stout cord. No doubt it was left there as a testament to others who had walked the same path as myself. I was not alone. Carefully, I measured the length from one looped end to the other. The cord would go around my neck and be threaded through the loop, and at the other end of the cord the loop would fit snugly around the narrow part of the wooden handle. The cord could be adjusted to suit whatever length was needed between my neck and the height of the bell at the dining table.

The evening meal arrived in the refectory and so did I, with the bell and cord at the ready. Grace was sung standing in lines facing one another, with me holding the bell by its clapper grasped firmly at my side. Sisters opposite glanced surreptitiously at the bell clasped in my hand. We sat down in our places. I placed the heavy bell on the table and adjusted the length of the cord around my neck. Our meal was served and I began to eat. As I took the first mouthful, the bell fell and clanged loudly and startled many of the other Sisters. Some held back grins fearing the same fate for them. This would never do. Well, I knew what I could do. Carefully I adjusted the cord to ensure the bell sat on the table, without moving when I took a mouthful.

The week of meals passed by and with careful adjustment of the cord length, I managed to keep the bell fully supported on the table surface, without allowing it to ring. Even the Novice Mistress did not seem to notice that it was not ringing as it could have been at my every mouthful. Maybe she had other distractions; watching her Postulants and Novices.

Soon the full week of 'bell' meals was over. During that time and in the ensuing weeks, I was careful to ring the bell faithfully on the dot of the appointed hour. Thus it was that I learnt during the remaining weeks a valuable lesson in time-keeping. I never again missed ringing the bell at the correct time. Punctuality in a convent is essential.

* * * * *

On an occasion when my time as bell ringer was over I was in the laundry when the bell calling Sisters to lunch rang. I hurried to the dining room. Standing in two rows facing one another as was the custom, we sang grace. As we stood with eyes downcast as was required, my eyes were distracted by an object held in the hands of one of the Senior Novices. I was unable to resist stealing a peek. Obviously the bell had caught her in the act of ironing, so she brought the iron in her hand, obeying the bell, or 'call of God', immediately. There were quite a few stifled giggles that day.

* * * * *

If I'd known that as a Franciscan nun, I would have to beg for what was needed, I think I would have reconsidered my choice to be a nun. I learned about the begging when I became a Novice.

One day Mother Bernadette sent for me. 'Sister, tomorrow we will go to London where we will visit some of the wholesale markets.'
'That will be a new experience for me, Mother.' We were going to London to get food for ourselves and our nursing home patients. Personally, I hated the idea of begging, but when one has taken the Vow of Obedience, there is no discussion, no argument.
'We leave at 6.00 pm tomorrow and will spend the night at Bishop's House, then in the morning we will drive straight to Smithfield Market, after which we will go on to Covent Garden Market. This will be a good lesson to learn Sister. I hope you'll enjoy it.'

We recited in unison the prayer *Memorare* as we left the gates of the Nursing Home, Mount Alvernia. This was a FMDM's custom as we drove anywhere, be it a short or a long journey. It was a prayer for safety under all circumstances, at all times. We travelled in an Austin van with Mother Bernadette driving.

We wore our cloaks over our habits and cardigans. It was a cold morning and we were grateful for the warmth inside the van. We could see the sun peeping over the hills on the east side of town as we drove along. The journey took about an hour and was made without speaking, it still being the Great Silence. When we reached the outskirts of London, we stopped briefly for a 'comfort' stop and we sat at a picnic table to eat some of our sandwiches and drink hot coffee. This was breakfast before we started our work of begging for supplies of food for our Nursing Home.

'Just follow my example, Sister. Get an empty sack from the back of the van and stand in front of the stall you want goods from. Just stand there until the stall

33

owner acknowledges you. Go up to him and give him the sack. He will take it away, fill it and when he returns, thank him for his generosity and take it back to the van, pack it in as far as you can reach. Pick up another empty sack and do the same at the next stall. That is how we do it.' We returned to the van and headed for the East End of London. Smithfield Market dealing in wholesale meats, covered many blocks and presented dark grey outer walls with stone colored pillars at intervals. We could see it was filling up quickly with people. There were buyers for hotels, restaurants, cafés, large and small establishments who came here to buy in bulk and at lower prices. We came to beg for our nursing home patients, and ourselves.

Mother Bernadette parked the van near an entrance door.
'Just follow me and watch what I do for the first few vendors, then you can start approaching them on your own.' I nodded and we entered the market precincts; thrown into the deep end so to speak. Firstly, we approached a vendor selling boxed beef and stood in front of his booth for a few minutes. He was serving a customer. When he finished, he turned and smiled at us.
'Good morning, Sisters, what can I do for you?'
'We'd be grateful for any meat you can spare for our nursing home,' answered Mother Bernadette. We waited whilst he searched his stock.
'Thirty pounds of good beef there. God bless you.' He handed a large box to me. We replied in unison, 'And God bless you for your generosity.' Mother instructed me to take the box back to the van. We then walked on to another vendor.

We watched the next vendor as he dealt with several customers. When he turned and came in our direction.

'What can I do for you, Sisters?' Mother Bernadette smiled at him.
'Anything for our nursing home would be much appreciated. He turned and searched his wares, and gave us a large package of pork. Before long we had chickens and from the fish section of the market we were given flounders and cod.

Mother said we would now go to Covent Garden to get vegetables. After driving across London we arrived at Covent Garden, a much bigger and brighter place with many different vendors with stalls displayed to show their wares; it was more like a Farmer's Market or a village fair with decorated stalls. Vegetables, fruits and flowers were the main wares and what a spread it was.

We repeated our routine at various stalls and came back to the van with sacks filled with cauliflowers, cabbages, potatoes, bananas, apples, oranges and even some nectarines, plums and pears. I found the generosity of the vendors quite amazing. I had no idea that this was how we shopped for food for our nursing home. I had no idea that this was how the Sisters went to market! The van was filled with evidence of this generosity.

To keep you safe when traveling.

The Memorare Prayer

Lord, be our guide and our protector
on the journey we are about to take.
Watch over us.
Protect us from accidents.
Keep us free from harm to body and soul.
Lord, support us with Your grace when we are tired.
Help us be patient in any trouble
which may come our way.
Keep us always mindful of Your presence and love.

Amen

6

Seeing the Sights

Mother General called me into her office. Being a first year Novice, I wondered why. Novices usually dealt directly with the Novice Mistress, not with the Foundress and Mother General. Inevitably, I thought just one word 'trouble.' Entering her office and standing in her hallowed presence, I waited to be spoken to.

'Sister Regina Mundi, I have a nice surprise for you. Remember I promised you would see Ireland even though you're going to be training in London? Well, I've arranged with Mother Superior at Portiuncula Hospital in Ballinasloe Ireland that you will spend six months with them and then return to Guildford. It will give you a chance to see the Irish countryside and experience the people you deal with, while you help Sister Evangelista in the physiotherapy department there.'

She studied my face, awaiting my reaction.
'That's exciting, Mother. Working in another country in one of our own hospitals and seeing the Irish countryside, who could ask for more?'

'You will need to take your personal clothing and necessities. We have arranged for you to fly from Gatwick to Dublin where you will be met by Sister Stanislaus, who you will report to while you are in Ireland. She and Sister Barbara will drive you to Galway. Now go make your preparations, as you leave tomorrow morning. Mother Andrew will let you know the time you need to be ready to be driven to Gatwick by two of our Sisters so you can board your flight. Off you go.'
'Thank you so much Mother, I look forward to this fascinating adventure.' I knelt for her blessing before leaving her room. She made the sign of the Cross on my forehead and I was free to leave.

Early next morning I stood in the foyer of our nursing home ready to leave Mount Alvernia Nursing Home at the top of the hill on Harvey Road in Guildford. Mother Andrew the Novice Mistress, and another Novice, Sister de la Lacrime, collected me and we boarded the van to Gatwick Airport about twenty miles away.

The Sisters escorted me to the check-in counter, said their goodbyes and left. Once on the plane and on the way to Dublin, I wondered what lay ahead of me. I had heard so much about Ireland and its people when chatting at recreation with the Irish Sisters that I was excited at the prospect of seeing the Emerald Isle. We flew for about two hours and the plane dipped as we circled to land at Dublin Airport. Looking out the window I spotted two Sisters standing at the Waving Gallery watching the plane land. At the sight of them I felt safe and knew everything was going to be all right. The excitement built as I strode along the corridor and arrived at Immigration and Customs. I passed through easily as the only thing in my possession was a small suitcase with my personal clothing and breviary.

Walking into the arrival hall, I saw the two Sisters waving and smiling a welcome to me. Sisters Stanislaus and Sister Barbara were welcoming and hugged me. Sister Stanislaus asked, 'How was your trip over, Sister?'

'Very pleasant, Sister,' I replied as we walked to the car. Looking around the building we had just exited, I noticed the green hues around me. 'Truly the Emerald Isles,' I said with admiration.

'And do you know why?' Sister Stanislaus asked. 'We have so much rain here that everything around us is green and bursting with life.'

'Reminds me so much of Malaysia and Singapore where the tropical rains have the same effect on the land.'

On our drive west from Dublin to Ballinasloe in County Galway the Sisters pointed out various places of interest. I loved listening to the Irish brogue as the Sisters continued to explain the surrounding countryside to me. Strong as the accent was, I found it quite easy to understand.

We arrived in Ballinasloe and drove around the Portiuncula Hospital to the building at the rear which was occupied by the Community of Sisters. For the next six months I too would live, eat and sleep in this building, and I would work in the hospital building in front of it.

I was assigned to help in the physiotherapy department and then help on the general wards with nursing. Often I was asked to 'prep' patients who came in for emergency operations. On one occasion a 'tinker' or Irish gypsy arrived in for an emergency appendix surgery. I was asked to prepare him for surgery which would be in our Operating Theatre. Gypsies did not always have access to bathing facilities, so the basic thing was to ensure he had a good hot bath and scrubbed the dirt away. I took him to the bathroom, put the plug into the outlet in the bath, started the hot and cold water taps, tested the temperature of the bath water and turned to the man.

'Liam, feel the water and if it's OK, there is soap there and a flannel here. When the water reaches a level suitable to you, turn it off and enjoy your bath. Don't forget to turn off the taps before the water fills the bath.' Leaving him in the bath I left, closing the bathroom door behind me.

A short time later, I heard water flowing. Rushing to the bathroom I saw water seeping under the door. I splashed through the water to turn off the taps which were running at full blast. The tinker sat in the bath, not moving a finger. It was obvious he had not scrubbed himself and seemed lost in his own world.

I fetched thick towels to soak up the excess water, having just averted a major disaster of flooded hospital corridors. Once that was seen to, I helped Liam out of the bath. Throughout the excitement, he had remained quiet and seemingly unaware of the commotion he had caused. I wondered if he was not all there: for not doing something about the water pouring over the sides of his bath.

Next on the agenda was to shave Liam in preparation for his emergency appendix operation. The rule back then was a person about to have an appendix operation had to be shaved from nipple level to the level of the knees. I had come equipped with six shaving razors. Systematically I worked down the front of his body from the nipples to his knees. His growth of hair was profuse and in no time at all, six blades were used. Shaving Liam was somewhat embarrassing for me, but as there were no secular males at the hospital, I was delegated the job. I was able to advise

Sister-in-Charge that the deed was done and he was ready for his operation; clean and shaved.

* * * * *

In the Convent the only ones I could have recreation with were the Postulants. I found this a bit boring as they were mostly young and from the country. Having enjoyed living in Perth and been something of a 'city slicker' prior to my religious life I was used to more mature company. However I fitted in wherever I happened to be and so I made the effort to be part of this group. One advantage was that the turnover of Postulants was such that constantly new girls arrived.

Ballinasloe was a training hospital for Nurses and Midwives and many Malaysian and Irish women and our order of nuns came here to train.

The daily routine for me would be first reporting to Sister Evangelista to check her workload and how much she needed me to help. If not needed by her, I would check with each of the floors; maternity, surgical, and medical and if not needed I could return to the Convent to do my daily prayer schedule, half an hour of meditation, half an hour of spiritual reading and Stations of the Cross.

I had been told to report to Sister Stanislaus weekly but I did not have an empathy with her. I felt an aversion to sharing my feelings with her. She didn't comment on my avoidance, and didn't call me in, so I just went on my own way. It was a Mexican stand off!

Time passed quickly and it was time for me to return to England and the Novitiate. I realised that I had not seen anything of the countryside and that was something I had looked forward to doing.

Sister Stanislaus called me into her office and said that arrangements had been made for my travel to Belfast as I would be boarding the ferry that runs between Belfast in Northern Ireland to Liverpool in England. She added that traveling with me would be two life-size statues and two large rolls of carpet, and two large trunks full of articles for the new Chapel being built at Ladywell Convent in Godalming, Surrey. These were packed into the van that would take us to Belfast. I was to lie down alongside the carpets and statues. It was from this position that I 'saw' the countryside of Ireland; such was the Vow of Obedience.

By not fulfilling my obligation of seeing Sister Stanislaus each week I knew it would go against me. I nevertheless was pleased to get away and back to the Novitiate and the other Novices I knew so well. I packed my few belongings in the small suitcase, said my goodbyes and left Ballinasloe.

The overnight ferry trip was horrendous; the tumultuous Irish Sea between Ireland and England caused me to be really unwell. Arriving at Liverpool, the next morning I was weak and disinterested in anything but going to bed, but I noted with a sinking feeling the two Sisters on the wharf waiting to take me back to Guildford.

It was a cold English day and after the van was loaded with the carpets, statues, and trunks, they bundled me in to lie flat along the length of the van, my small suitcase beside me, with my head just behind the nun who drove to Guildford. Again I was being transported as freight; such is the Vow of Obedience.

The next day I was called into a meeting with Mother General. Because I had not reported to Sister Stanislaus each week for my separate lesson where I was to discuss my innermost thoughts, I would have to leave the convent. This was considered major disobedience. I had felt no connection with her during my time in Ireland so had been unable to confide in her. I was instructed by Mother General to write a letter to my parents to tell them that I had to leave the convent due to ill health.

'But I do not have ill health, Mother!'

'You will do as you are told, Sister. You will go and write that letter to your parents immediately.' I turned and left her room, feeling incensed at what seemed to me unjust treatment, and a lie, too. I pondered on why an untruth was necessary.

Next day when summoned, I walked in and handed over the letter. Mother Francis carefully read it.

'Sister, I have changed my decision on this matter. This letter no longer needs to be sent to your parents. You will be given another chance and allowed to complete your Noviciate in July 1956 as originally planned. We will watch your behaviour and God willing there will not be a repeat of what happened in Ballinasloe. Now go, with my blessing, and start over.' With these words, she blessed me and smiled her dismissal. I felt frustrated by this episode. I put it behind me and tried to be a good nun.

Of all the things we as Novices were asked to do, I found the weekly visit to our Novice Mistress Mother Andrew hard on my psyche. I found it difficult to discuss my innermost thoughts and feelings about the life we were expected to lead: training for the three Vows of Poverty, Chastity and Obedience along with the rule of Silence.

I thought further on the religious life and the demands on my humanity and strength of character. I lectured myself; 'Well Esmé, you knew life inside was not going to be easy. Now at the first difficulty you are finding it hard to accept the demands in the religious life. Pull up your socks and throw yourself wholeheartedly into doing as you are told, and that should be a good start to changing your life and its pathway. Make the effort to be as good as you can. You will be given the courage and strength through God's grace.'

Decision made, I felt somewhat stronger and able to go on with firm resolve.

* * * * *

Laudate Jesus Christus; Praise Jesus Christ. A voice in what seemed the middle of the night rang out. I sat up, checked my watch and saw it was 4:30 am on a crisp autumnal morning. In spite of the early hour birds cheeped merrily in the garden of the suburban house in which twenty young Franciscan nuns slept. We worked across the road at Mount Alvernia Nursing Home, which was run and staffed by our nuns in Guildford, Surrey.

It was from the Motherhouse that Sisters, who had taken their Vows and trained in varying careers, went out as Missionaries to Africa, the Far East and Europe. In England they worked in orphanages and homes for unmarried mothers, and at this Nursing Home, where they admitted surgical, medical and maternity patients under the care of doctors.

Hurrying out of my cubicle, to the end of the aisle between two rows of nun's cubicles I picked up the tall enamel jug filled with hot water for our ablutions. I

44

poured some into my basin which was on the upended orange box which served as a locker. Overnight as the temperature plummeted the face flannels, spread out to dry on the bottom of the upturned wash basins, froze and assumed the shape of the basin. Returning the jug to its place so other Sisters could have hot water, I hurried back to my cell to complete my ablutions.

The temperature this morning did nothing to help my fingers move, as I dressed in my nun's clothing. We wore outer cloaks buttoned down the front from neck to hem to protect our white habit and for warmth, of course.

Ten of us assembled in the foyer of the Mount Alvernia Nursing Home preparatory to walking down the hill to the Guilford railway station to catch the 'workingman's run' to Waterloo Station on the south bank of the Thames River in London. The train journey from London Road to Waterloo Station took an hour and we arrived in time to eat our picnic breakfast of sandwiches and thermos coffee before we boarded the tube to Trafalgar Square.

The centre for collectors was in the Crypt of St Martin-in-the-Fields Church in Trafalgar Square. Each person was given a box of flags and a tin with a hole in the lid for donations, together with a tag identifying us as collectors. The leader of the group then assigned us to various points around Piccadilly Circus, and the streets running off the Circus.

Standing at our posts at various points around Piccadilly Square in exchange for a donation we offered flags to the people walking past. Most people were generous. We heard many different languages spoken as people hurried by, showing that even in the late fifties London was full of people from throughout Europe, and the world.

Every year a group of nuns helped on Flag Day for Saint Barnardo's Homes for Children in and around London. The flag was the size of a postage stamp with a pin stuck through. Our order ran a home for unwanted babies and children from birth to six years in Chislehurst Kent, and an orphanage for children from seven to sixteen in Aldershot. We were given a percentage of the funds we collected in London towards the upkeep of these two homes.

Mid-morning, lunch-time and mid-afternoon we returned to St Martin-in-the-Fields for tea or coffee, a snack and a brief rest. Following the fifteen minute break, we returned to a different location to sell the flags.

We finished selling at 6.00 pm and by that time I was so tired that instead of saying the usual 'Would you buy a flag?' I heard myself say, 'Would you flag a buy?'

* * * * *

It was part of our training as Novices to do a short stint at our smaller Nursing Home for Elders called La Verna, which was also located in Godalming, Surrey. It was acceptable for the nuns to use the patient's bathrooms in the Nursing Home before retiring to sleep in our simple huts located in the grounds. Sleeping accommodation for the nuns was sparse and in the true sense of Franciscan Poverty with little or no insulation of the building. So a warm bath or shower was greatly appreciated in the winter months, especially for those of us who had previously lived in tropical climes.

One evening after a shower in one of the patient's bathrooms, which we were permitted to use, I made my way to our separate accommodation clad in just a nightshirt and night guimpe; similar to a balaclava but in cotton material. I walked out of the area where the bathrooms and sluice rooms were located.

Visiting hours were long over. Out of the blue I came face to face with a beautiful lady, dressed impeccably, who smiled at me.
'Good night, Sister.' I quickly murmured a reply as she disappeared out of sight. Then like a bolt of lightning the penny dropped. That lady was none other than Deborah Kerr, actress and movie star! Her mother was one of our patients and I guessed that rather than meet hordes of fans, she preferred to visit her mother in privacy and quiet in the later hours.

Excitement raced through my body as I realised who it had been. For years I had admired this beautiful actress and that year, 1956, her latest film was released; *Anna and the King of Siam* with Yul Brynner and it had topped the charts as a musical. I realised I had missed the chance to rub shoulders with the famous!

A fleeting moment in time and one I have treasured always as a happy memory.

Deborah Kerr

Seven Decade Rosary

7

First Vows and Life as a Young Blue Veil

Two years had passed and in July 1956 I along with seven of my sisters took our First Vows. We had been deemed suitable to make our 'First Profession of Vows'. This took place at Ladywell Convent in Godalming, about eight miles from Guildford's Mt Alvernia Nursing Home where we worked. A new Chapel at Ladywell was being built; it was officially opened in 1962. A large room in the main building at Ladywell Convent was used as a temporary Chapel in the meantime. We were the first group to take our vows at Ladywell.

At this solemn ceremony I made my Vows and was given a silver medal of Our Lady on a blue cord to wear around my neck. I received a Blue Veil to signify the next stage of my religious life which I would wear over my daily white veil when I entered the Chapel each morning and evening. On my head was placed a Crown of Flowers which I wore for that day. I was now referred to as a 'YBV', Young Blue Veil.

Official photographs were taken outside in the garden close to where the Chapel was being built. Copies of the photographs were sent to my family; the first contact that they had with me for two years.

* * * * *

Several months before my First Professional Vows at the Motherhouse at Godalming, Surrey, Mother Francis called me to her office. 'Sister, now we need to decide which training you want to do. Do you wish to train as a doctor, physiotherapist, nurse or midwife or anything else needed in our hospital in Singapore? All our homes, nursing homes and hospitals are self-sufficient with preferably sisters being in charge of all departments in whatever line of work we do. Do you have a preference for the work you want to do?'

'I have thought about this, Mother. The work I most like to do is physiotherapy. I have been told I have healing hands and I would like to use them to help people in pain and suffering.'

'We've had several sisters who trained in physiotherapy, including your Mistress of Novices, Mother Andrew. Our Sisters who do physiotherapy train at the St Thomas' Physiotherapy School in London which keeps a place for one of our Sisters when they have a new intake of students. So Sister, all being well, the new term starts in September. I will apply for you to start then. In the meantime you will stay on in Guildford and do whatever Mother Bernadette asks of you.'

I loved being at our Mount Alvernia Nursing Home at Guildford, which was eight miles away from the Motherhouse at Godalming; we admitted medical, surgical and maternity patients, so there was ample scope to practise what I already knew of physiotherapy treatments. During my first years as a nun Mother Andrew had taught me the various physiotherapy treatments and she allowed me to perform treatments on patients.

* * * * *

Following the Divine Office on Friday evening, the Community of Sisters, would move silently from the Chapel to the Refectory for the weekly Chapter of Faults.

Fridays for nuns who had taken Vows, was the day chosen to 'confess' our faults to the Superior, in the presence of the whole community. It took place in the Refectory, a large room sparsely furnished. Standing around the walls were the Sisters ranging from the most junior near the entry door, to the most senior Sisters near the Superior.

This weekly practice was regarded as a way to humiliate us and train us in the practice of humility and the self abasement of our character. At this stage, none of us knew how the others felt about these practices because of the Rule of Silence. We could never debate the pros and cons with our superiors because we were never asked, nor were we offered the opportunity to say anything on this subject.

When everyone assembled in order of superiority, the Superior intoned a brief prayer and then gave the signal for the Chapter of Faults to begin. The most junior Sister moved into the centre aisle, knelt down, stating her faults loud enough for all to hear. Some would confess about breakages in their work, some would mention being unkind to another Sister, others would admit to minor sins of offense, omission, or oversight.

The Mother Superior acknowledged the confession, gave an appropriate brief admonition. The humiliated Sister got up and returned to her place at the back of the room. This would be repeated until we had all completed our confessions. The Superior then gave thanks with a few prayerful words.

In the privacy of our cells, we would pull our habit off one shoulder, pick up The Discipline, made of knotted cotton cords and commence to whip ourselves. Holding it at one end by the large knot, I used it in self flagellation for about ten minutes, at the same time murmuring requests for forgiveness, for the faults I had confessed to at Chapter. After some weeks of this, I got bored with this activity and used to make the noise with my fingernails without the actual self flagellation. I thought to myself 'this is a silly practice and totally unnecessary.' No one checked on us or mentioned anything. So I got away with it.

If done correctly the Discipline or Cat o' Nine Tails is an instrument for causing pain and possibly marks as well. This was an ancient form of torture for monks and nuns which put them in mind of the whipping Jesus suffered before his Crucifixion. His whipping cords caused blood to flow. What we used was minor in comparison.

After this form of self torture, I would then retire to bed and waken the next day to whatever life brought me.

* * * * *

Since arriving in England I had dreamed that by hook or by crook I was going to have a hot bath in one of the patient's bathrooms in the Mount Alvernia Nursing Home. These bathrooms spent most of their time unused though Novices cleaned them regularly every week. I had decided, despite rules and reason, that whatever happened I was going to have a lovely hot bath. The bathroom I chose was on the third floor, out of the way of the usual traffic at that time in the evening.

After my delicious bath I carefully tucked my wet towel under my apron and made my way back to my quarters. I had fulfilled my dream, but unfortunately not without Mother Margaret meeting me as I walked along the corridor.

First Professed or Young Blue Veils, YBV's, as we were now called, were spiritually guided by Mother Margaret, Vicaress General of the Congregation. Mother Margaret was well known as a real stickler for discipline and obedience.

She stared at the growing wet spot at my belly and demanded, 'Sister, what have you been doing in this area so late at night?' Ever truthful I told her that I had been having a bath in the bathroom at the end of maternity floor. Her eyes flew wide open and in clipped tones she said, 'I will deal with you tomorrow morning at lesson, Sister,' and walked haughtily away.

The next morning at lesson she demanded I come to the centre of the room, kneel on the carpet and I had to describe to the class what I had done. She then verbally wiped the floor with me and gave me a penance of scrubbing the scullery and kitchen floors each day for a week. These were by nature of the work done in those areas, the dirtiest floors in the hospital.

A few weeks later when Mother Francis visited Mount Alvernia Nursing Home I was summoned to meet with her and Mother Margaret in the room where I usually conducted physiotherapy treatments.

I entered the room and knelt for Mother Francis' blessing as customary. When I stood up again Mother Margaret said, 'Mother, Sister Regina Mundi will never be alone wherever she is. If she goes to Heaven, a hundred people will be with her. If she goes to hell, a hundred people will be with her! There is no doubt Sister has a powerful effect on all who come in contact with her.' Mother Margaret then launched into an account of my misbehavior. My eyes were downcast as they were supposed to be, but for one moment when I glanced up, I could see Mother Francis' twinkling eyes. I knew I had an ally!

I was pleasantly surprised when Mother Francis replied, 'Don't you think we need more Sisters like Sister Regina Mundi, with her passion and spirit and innovative thinking?' Mother Margaret's jaw dropped. Turning to me Mother Francis said, 'I'm sure you learnt a valuable lesson Sister, and in future you will think twice before you repeat any transgression.'
Mother Francis's generous spirit saved me and I felt I had learnt a lesson which inspired me to try harder to be a better Sister and keeper of the Vows of Poverty, Chastity and Obedience.

* * * * *

Eight week old puppies jostled each other along the corridor as their mother Sally nuzzled them to the door leading out to the back garden of the hospital. A picture I found hard to forget. Sally was training her young ones to use the garden instead of their litter box. Two pups were fully black and the other six were golden replicas of their mother; all had the unmistakable square heads so distinctive in Labradors.

Apart from treating in-patients with their physiotherapy needs as directed by Mother Andrew, additional responsibilities for me in Guildford were to keep the Chapel and Sacristy and large Refectory clean, for the daily use of the Community of Sisters at meal and prayer times. I operated the laundry equipment for the hospital linen, diapers from the maternity floor and the community laundry. Last but definitely not least, it was my duty to look after Sally, the golden Labrador who was the Nursing Home dog. Sally and I had a good relationship, but when I was away carrying out my other duties, she got restless and often wandered out of the hospital grounds.

Mount Alvernia Nursing Home stood at the top of a steep hill rising up from the end of the main street in Guildford town. Back then the main street remained cobbled, but Harvey Road leading off the main street to the nursing home was asphalt. Snow fell thickly in winter and the roads often iced overnight, which proved dangerous especially on a gradient of forty five degrees.

Chasing after Sally whenever she wandered off, often meant my slipping and sliding down the hill instead of walking with the appropriate dignity for which our Sisters were well known. A young nun with black cloak flying, as she pursued her wandering dog down the hill, ending in the main street of the town was a sight for the people of Guildford to stop and smile.

On one of these occasions, Sally wandered, fortuitously as it turned out, into the grounds of the home of one of the surgeons who was a consultant to our nursing home. His male Labrador was black and in no time, the deed was done and Sally happily returned to the haven of our nursing home.

In time, Sally became larger and larger until early one morning I arrived at my physiotherapy room to find her in a large cardboard carton lying on her side, six babies suckling and five more lying around the box. The Night Sister-in-Charge, Sister Richard arrived to explain. Sister Richard a midwife had noticed on her night rounds that Sally had started to produce her puppies around midnight. She placed Sally in the box and kept a watchful eye from then on. By morning eleven puppies had arrived but some were weaker than others. The vet was called and she examined mother and pups and immediately put three of the weakest into her pockets. She advised that Sally was too young at just a year old, to have a litter of eleven. Sally was left with eight puppies, two were totally black like their father, and the remaining six were golden, like their mother.

Despite being young, Sally proved to be a natural mother who trained her puppies to use the litter box indoors and when they were ready to venture further she guided them along the corridors to the door leading out to the back garden. This was amazing to behold; watching them tumble down the two steps and on to the grass.

When the pups were ten weeks old people lined up to give them a good home. By this time they were delightful Labrador puppies and we found homes for them all, which left Sally alone again. Having had one litter seemed to settle Sally down, and the wander-lust episodes ceased.

It was time to leave for London to commence physiotherapy training. I said goodbye to Sally and the Sisters at Mount Alvernia, Guildford and with my suitcase, boarded the train to Waterloo, and a new life as a training Sister in London.

* * * * *

Travel by British Rail in the fifties was fast. During the week I was one of three Franciscan Sisters living at Bishop's House London. On Friday evening we took the fast train from London to return to the Motherhouse, Ladywell Convent in Godalming, Surrey. This particular weekend it was a long weekend with Monday being a public holiday. The three of us looked forward to country life, after experiencing life in busy London.

One evening at recreation we learned that for the next two days our assignment was to dig out the area where a new swimming pool was to be built. The media had been notified by our Mother General who considered all publicity essential to encourage new women to join our Order, and a news team was coming to film 'Franciscan Nuns Digging Their Own Swimming Pool.' We were going to be famous, or so we thought!

Next morning we donned our blue aprons and set out to start digging. One of the senior Sisters arrived escorting the film crew. The man operating the large movie camera asked us to carry on with what we were doing and they would commence filming. They told us that in a few days time, what they had recorded would be a Pathé News item on the television and in cinemas. The team would return when the pool and surrounds were built and landscaped to complete the story.

That night at recreation the chatter was on the subject of Ladywell being on Pathé News. Reverend Mother Leonard told us that Pathé would advise when we were to be on their television news.

After two days of digging we had the Monday of our long weekend off, to recover enough to return to our teaching and physiotherapy classes on Tuesday. It seemed that every muscle in my body was aching after two days of digging.

The following week we heard that our pool digging was to be on the television news on Friday evening. Fortunately the time coincided with our recreation which meant we would be able to view it. We collected in the recreation room and sat down to wait for the 'Nuns Dig Pool' story. It opened with a view of our long front drive lined with daffodils on each side. The drive led to the front entry of the Main House. The commentary announced that this was the Motherhouse of Franciscan nuns who ran nursing homes, shelters for unmarried mothers expecting their babies and hospitals in the United Kingdom, Ireland, Africa, America and the Far East. 'These nuns are self-sufficient in all they do.' The commentator went on to say, 'They even dig their own swimming pool.' The picture moved to the dig site and there we were, hard at work.

The Sisters cheered when they saw themselves on the screen. The commentator finished off by saying it was the start of the project and there would be a second visit when they hoped to show views of the finished swimming pool, the changing rooms beside the pool, and the landscaped gardens.

The changing rooms would have an external cladding of Bargate stone from the Surrey countryside, and were a testament to the nuns who lifted the extremely heavy

58

pieces of stone to make those beautiful changing rooms. The stonework added greatly to the scene of a beautiful swimming pool complex.

I heard some years later that the area was returned to lawn, as the pool complex did not get sufficient use to justify the upkeep. A sad end to a beautiful pool, and I never had a swim!

Sister Regina Mundi 1961 after Final Vows
From Esmé's Photograph Album

8

Training Sister in London

Arrangements were made with the School of Physiotherapy, who notified the September starting date of the next intake. It was necessary to wear the uniform, so approval was sought from the Pope in Rome for the right to wear this uniform during my training time. This meant that I traveled to school in my nun's habit and changed into the uniform.

At classes we wore a divided beige skirt with a beige and white pinstriped blouse with a Peter Pan collar. For Greek dancing classes we wore a brown playsuit which was worn for other practical classes similar to massage. When we needed to move over to the hospital ten minutes down the road, we wore brown cloaks over our uniforms with beige cross-over straps to differentiate us from the nurses who wore navy blue cloaks with red cross-over straps in front.

* * * * *

As nuns, we had a host of prayers, odds and ends to do before our actual working day began. Suffice to say, this Monday morning I was running later than usual; I was endeavouring to 'rev' my pace up so I could get down to the railway station to catch my weekly commute from Guildford to London. Looking at the time I realised I needed to move fast, so hurriedly I put on my cloak and veil.

Picking up my small suitcase with my physiotherapy uniform and books inside, I flew out the front door of the nursing home, down the steep incline of Harvey Road to the city making sure I didn't fall. Reaching the bottom of the hill I then turned right and headed to the railway station at London Road.

Breathing fast, I reached the top of the staircase leading down to the railway track where my commute train sat, waiting to take off exactly on the dot according to the timetable.

I wasn't sure whether I would reach the train before it took off but I noticed the stationary train had steam puffing out the funnel above the engine.

Can I make it I wondered? The next available train would make me late for Physiotherapy School. Fortunately, the school was beside Waterloo Station. Once I arrived at Waterloo, it was just a hop, step and a jump to the school.

Then, I noticed that the train driver was leaning out the window giving me the thumbs up; he was obviously waiting for me to board! As fast as I could, but being careful, I descended the old wooden staircase to the level of the railway tracks. The station master was holding a carriage door open for me. I bounded up the steps and burst into the railway carriage. As I did so, a loud cheer rang out from the passengers and immediately the train started to roll and quickly picked up speed. Not the most elegant behaviour for a young nun, but the important thing was I had caught my usual train to the big city.

What amazed me was the hearty cheer from all and sundry; these were people who normally had their eyes glued to the morning paper or a book, and they didn't say boo to a goose. The English are well known for their 'stiff upper lip' and all that, but I realised that on this occasion I was known and recognized. So all was well that ended well. I had an exciting tidbit to share with my fellow students at our morning break.

* * * * *

Arriving at our Physiotherapy School in good time for the first lecture, I walked into the Change Room with a row of about ten toilets and entered one. I locked the door and put my suitcase on the seat. I transferred the contents from the body of the case to the lid, and as I removed my nun's clothes, put them in the suitcase.

I put on the uniform. First the gym costume, then the 'skort', a divided skirt, then the blouse, in the colours of brown, beige and cream, the colours of the School of Physical Therapy. I changed the white stockings for the skin-colored stockings that were uniform. The cloak the Physiotherapy students wore outside in the elements was dark brown with a beige cross-over holding it in place.

During the time I was changing, I heard calls from my fellow students standing outside, 'Hurry up Sister, we want to use the toilet.' My reply was, there are other toilets: use one of them!

When I was dressed, I stepped out of the toilet and almost knocked over the line of my teasers. I walked out smiling, put my case in my locker and grabbing my books and my brown cloak headed for the first class of the day.

* * * * *

The main subjects in Physical Therapy as it was then known were anatomy, physiology and electro-mechanics. These were the subjects we learned for eighteen months before we took the first important examination; Preliminary. This was all theory and it was necessary to pass before going on to the next level; which took a year's study. The Intermediate examination was half theory and half practical. Six months later, we would sit the Final examination which was all practical; practical treatments for different types of injuries and conditions using massage, exercises and electro-mechanical treatments.

The first time I sat the Preliminary examination, I was extremely nervous and when I read the questionnaire, I could only answer the bare necessities, not enough for a proper answer. I panicked, I couldn't think. I handed in the paper knowing it was insufficient. When the results came out, my fears were realised. I had not passed. I was devastated - never in my life until now had I failed an examination. I was mortified.

My lecturer explained that in order to do the examination again, it meant going down to the group below and re-sitting the examination in six months time. This I did and repeated the classes that I had done before. But once again I failed. The lecturer advised that it was possible to re-sit the examination, but I would have to do the six months yet again.

Six months later I sat the Preliminary examination for the third time. Weeks later I received the results to find that once again I had failed to make the grade. Feeling very upset and dejected, I informed our Mother General back in Guildford. She asked me to return to Guildford. I did willingly. Meantime she contacted my teachers at St Thomas' and they told her that they too could not understand why I had failed the same examination three times as I was the best student in my group each time and it showed in the practical subjects that were based on the theory learnt. I was devastated that after three attempts I still could not pass the first examination in Physiotherapy training.

Mother Francis said to me, 'Sister, it's not possible to repeat the examinations again so come back and work in Guildford with Mother Bernadette for a couple of months. Then it will be time to return to Singapore. In the meantime, write out a list of equipment you would need to start a physiotherapy department in our planned new Singapore Hospital. You will have a room big enough to take all your equipment and three treatment plinths. That should be a good start for the new hospital.' This was an amazing reward considering I wasn't qualified. Sister Francis knew my practical work was of a high standard.

Two weeks before Christmas 1959 I was called into Mother Francis office once again. 'Sister, you will pack your personal belongings as I am sending you to Italy for a ten day holiday with our Sisters at Collegio Beda. You are booked to sail from Naples to Singapore after Christmas, and due to arrive in Singapore in the New Year. The other two Sisters going with you are Sister Aquinas and Sister Marie Louise. You will be able to visit Assisi when you are in Rome and learn more about Saint Francis and Saint Clare. You will find that quite an experience.'

I was overjoyed at this good news and my drooping spirits immediately came alive with hope and a sense that we would enjoy our visit to Rome and Assisi. I asked Mother Francis if we could get off the liner at Colombo, as I had many relations living there who wanted to meet me. Mother agreed as long as we, the three Sisters remained together.

We had a farewell at our Motherhouse in Surrey before we left on our journey back to Singapore. From London to Paris we crossed the Channel on the Night Ferry, and then on to Rome, by train.

Before I relate the stories of my return to Singapore, I'll tell you about Sister Rosa Mystica, an Irish lass who was great fun. She provided us with laughter and many happy memories.

9

Sister Rosa Mystica

While walking the seven minutes home at the end of a day to the convent Bishop's House in Southwark, where London based training Sisters lived, I mulled over the impending visit of my friend due to arrive that evening for a night's stay. Three of our Sisters looked after the Bishop and the administration of Bishops House.

Sister Rosa Mystica would arrive in time for the evening meal and stay overnight. I remembered several funny occasions that occurred when we were in the Noviciate. Being Irish, Sister had a keen sense of humour in a typically Celtic way which was even more amusing to those of us from Malaysia and Singapore, than those who were English.

What could I do to 'welcome' her in the short space of time she spent with us. She was due to arrive in time for the evening meal, followed by an hour's recreation and then we were off to night prayers and bed. There was not much time but I was determined to do something.

I sat in our study room, going over the day's lectures and looking over my half skeleton and skull, basic requirements in my training as a physiotherapist, when a brilliant idea occurred. Rosa Mystica would take part in our activities but time to speak together semi-privately would not be available. Sitting there I realised that I could use one of my night guimpes. Excited at the thought of what I predicted would happen I took the skull out of its soft bag and walked to the bed where Sister Rosa Mystica would sleep. I set down the skull wearing my guimpe so it was resting on the pillow with the eye sockets facing the door into the room.

After recreation and night prayers, it was then the Great Silence during which time not a word was permitted, unless there was fire or haemorrhage, until after prayers, Mass and breakfast the next morning. This meant I would not speak to my friend as she would leave immediately after Mass the next morning for the markets, to beg for supplies for the nursing home and our Motherhouse.

We indicated with a note to Sister Rosa Mystica that she could use the bathroom first and repair to bed. She nodded and went off to the bathroom. Three of us who had study to do, sat waiting. We heard her footsteps from bathroom to bedroom and in the next moment a piercing scream shattered the Great Silence.

We waited in case Mother Superior appeared, so we carried on studying. I felt it best to remain where I was rather than rush to see why Sister Rosa Mystica had screamed; knowing full well why! The other two Sisters training as teachers, giggled. They were in on my prank. As I prepared for bed I found the skull on an empty bed and Sister Rosa Mystica fast asleep, or pretending to be. I collected the skull, put it away and retired to bed. Poor Sister Rosa Mystica was by then truly fast asleep.

We would not talk until the evening recreation the next day but we giggled and exchanged pointed looks.

* * * * *

Another incident involving Sister Rosa Mystica happened during our Novice days at La Verna, the small nursing home mainly for older people and where I had seen Deborah Kerr. Each morning one of us helped the Night Sister when she woke the patients in the morning. We would leave the Chapel to help her with whatever she wanted us to do whilst the Sisters chanted the Divine Office.

The Night Sister asked Sister Rosa Mystica to make sure the bed-bound patients were given bedpans and had a morning wash before they were served breakfast. She was reminded to make sure the bedpans were warmed before they were given to the patients.

For some reason Mother Bernadette had to leave the Chapel that morning and as she walked through the kitchen she was greeted by the sight of Sister Rosa Mystica inserting a bedpan into the kitchen oven. Despite it still being the Great Silence, Mother was forced to say, 'Sister, why are you putting that bedpan into the kitchen oven?'

Immediately the response came from Sister Rosa Mystica. 'I'm warming it, as Sister asked me to do, Mother.'

'Remove the bedpan immediately, Sister. Go to the sluice room and hold the pan under running hot water until it's warm. Never again bring a bedpan into the kitchen where food is prepared!' said Mother Bernadette as she proceeded to do what she had intended to do, before being distracted.

* * * * *

Another incident with Sister Rosa Mystica occurred whilst we were at La Verna. This time she was asked to relieve the Night Sister for the evening recreation. At the time of change-over the dangerous drugs are checked as these required counting and signing off by two Sisters at each patient's record and in the Drug Register. The Night Sister ran through the list and said she would sign the register on her return from recreation. She asked Sister Rosa Mystica to sign her column as checker. The next day at evening recreation the Night Sister told the community that on her return she went straight to the Dangerous Drug register to sign for the drugs she had checked with Sister Rosa Mystica. Sister found that not only had she signed the drugs they checked together, but she had gone on signing down the column, page after page until the end of the book!

The Night Sister chuckled as she remembered. 'So that is what Sister Rosa Mystica did during the whole hour of recreation.'

After Sister Rosa Mystica was Professed and started her training as a nurse, she sailed through each year with flying colours and she qualified not only top of her class in the hospital where she trained, but top of the nurses in the hospitals throughout England. Just goes to show that she wasn't as dumb as she would have us believe!

10

Return to Singapore

The three of us had travelled by train from London to Rome. The plan was for us to spend ten days in Rome before we caught the train from Rome to Naples, where we would board a liner leaving for our ultimate destination of Singapore.

In England for the past six years, Sister Louise Marie and I had completed our religious training and then trained in our chosen field; Sister Louise Marie had just completed her nursing diploma at our hospital in Ballinasloe, County Galway and I had trained but not passed Physiotherapy, but I was still regarded as an excellent physiotherapist.

Arrival in Rome was exciting as we watched the bustling traffic outside the railway station. Sister Mary Joseph from *Collegio Beda* met us and we loaded our luggage into the community's car. After the quick drive through the city scenery of many blocks of apartments and views of parks interspersed with the buildings, we arrived at Collegio Beda, a huge square edifice surrounded by a high wall. We passed through the gateway into an inner courtyard. We unloaded our luggage and were shown to our sleeping quarters.

It was the Christmas season. Each day of our ten day visit we acted as tourists, visiting the famous churches, cathedrals and museums dotted around the city, including the one next to the Collegio Beda, St Paul's Cathedral, and of course the Vatican; the Piazza San Pietro, St Peter's Cathedral the centre of Roman Catholic faith and the Sistine Chapel.

We kept one day aside for the train trip to Assisi. First we visited the Cathedral of Saint Francis of Assisi where we saw the magnificent frescoes, and the little Chapel in which Saint Francis received his stigmata; the wounds of Christ on the Cross.

We discovered that the Poor Clare monastery where Saint Francis had lived in his last years was a ten minute drive up a hill. So we hired a taxi which drove us up to the Poor Clare Convent. Did I say the taxi drove us? It was tearing up the narrow road of stones with a steep fall-away on one side. We heaved sighs of fervent relief when we reached the top of the Mount; here Saint Francis had slept in his own room on a bed of rock with a smaller rock as a pillow for his head. Outside in the garden just a few feet from his room stood the tree under which Saint Francis gave his famous sermon to the animals and birds of the area. That tree was eight hundred years old in 1960 when we saw it. It was supported by a solid steel girder as it grew out of the side of the hill.

Our return to the base of the mount was much more sedate and in fact we tipped the taxi driver generously for his safe driving. We could not have driven again with the previous taxi driver. To this day I don't remember where the money to pay for the taxi came from, but I presume Sister Aquinas had been given money to allow us to travel and eat when sightseeing.

Walking to the station to return to the city of Rome from Assisi, we passed two men sitting on the side of the road smoking. I felt a distinct pinch and twist of my bottom through my cloak. I immediately turned around and one man had the audacity to give me a wink and a thumbs up! He looked pleased with himself and I was angry. However, it seemed not the place to make a scene, so I closed my mouth and walked on. The other two Sisters seemed not to have had the same treatment, nor did they appear to have noticed what happened to me.

Oh well, I believe Italian peasants are known for this crude expression of approval of a woman.

* * * * *

Three nuns, a priest, and a doctor sat in deck chairs talking and laughing. I realise this sounds like the beginning of a joke! It's not a joke; but I learned more about myself. The top deck of this Italian liner was the best place to enjoy the fresh air, warm sun, and the company of fellow travelers. We exchanged stories and experiences of our years overseas.

We had boarded at Naples and would disembark at Singapore. Sister Marie Louise originally from Singapore was a similar age to me. We were returning to our homeland after six years of training in England, and the older senior nun accompanying us was Sister Aquinas from Ireland assigned to Singapore as Assistant to the Sister Superior there.

The young priest Father Peter grew up in Mainland China and after ten years in seminaries in Spain and Rome he spoke English with difficulty and with an Italian-Spanish accent. His Italian and Spanish were fluent as was his Latin and his own native dialect from Mainland China. He had completed his training in seminaries in Madrid and Rome. He was keen to learn as much conversational English as he could and asked if I would help. He had been assigned as Parish Priest in a small church in rural Malaysia. The fifth person was a very handsome young Pakistani who had gained his medical degree in England and then he specialised in surgery. He spoke Oxford English as he had spent his past ten years in various parts of England; at different universities as he progressed through the stages of his medical studies.

Father Peter hesitantly spoke, 'Sister, I am grateful that you will help me speak English better than I do. I need to understand what my parishioners say and I will have to reply to them. I don't know how I will write my sermons, but I'm sure the good Lord will help me.'
'We have time before we reach Singapore Father Peter, so I'm sure you will learn enough to be able to communicate with anyone you wish,' I replied and smiled at him.

Kareem the Pakistani doctor then asked, 'Can you explain how someone as beautiful as you Sister, decided to become a nun and live behind closed walls? It seems a strange choice to make.'
'I understand what you mean,' I replied, 'but if you think about it why should God choose the bad potatoes? If a man can choose the woman he wants, why not God who created us?'
'Touché,' Karem laughed. 'When you put it that way it's clear. I admire the work nuns do. They are totally devoted to their work.'
'We approach our work from a different angle. It's because we do our work for God; that is why we are so devoted to it, and for no other reason. Having taken

the three Vows of Poverty Chastity and Obedience, every action performed is for the glory of God.'

The other two Sisters had remained quiet through the exchange. Sister Aquinas now announced, 'Please excuse us, Gentlemen, we have some things to do,' and with that we took our leave. In our cabin Sister Aquinas expressed her concern.

'I'm not quite sure how to handle this situation, Sister Regina Mundi. I fear that our doctor Kareem shows more than a slight interest in you. I know you have not encouraged his attentions at all, but he seems interested. It is difficult to avoid meeting them, as our boat is not big and our journey takes at least sixteen days. We just need to think of a way to deal with this situation without resorting to extremes. Besides, we may be jumping to the wrong conclusion.' We agreed that I would be accompanied by one of my Sisters at all times. I was polite but avoided any prolonged conversation with him. He did try to strike up a conversation at every opportunity.

Fortunately this predicament was resolved when the handsome doctor disembarked at our first port of call, his home town of Karachi, Pakistan. Watching him disembark, I turned to Sister Aquinas and said, 'Phew!' breathing a sigh of relief. 'He was nice but becoming fixated and it is good to see him leave peaceably.' Sister agreed with me.

'You handled him well Sister, in spite of his avid interest.'

'Diplomacy,' I replied to Sister Aquinas, 'is not one of my strong points, but I try.'

Although I was pursued by the handsome Pakistani doctor during our trip from Naples through the Suez Canal I was strengthened in my realization that I had no physical attraction to Kareem or any other man, for that matter. It explained why in my dealings with men I remained objective. My heart didn't beat faster nor did I long to see him again, I just wasn't attracted to him. I was confident, I trusted my feelings, and I knew that they wouldn't change.

* * * * *

Christmas was celebrated at *Collegio Beda* and was followed a few days later with the three of us leaving Rome by train for Naples. We boarded the liner that took us to Singapore, with two stops on the way: Karachi in Pakistan, and Colombo in Sri Lanka. I had connected with relations in Colombo who wished to show us around the city and insisted we enjoy a typical Dutch Burgher lunch with them. The ship was going to be docked until nightfall, so that gave us the day to spend with my cousins whom I had not met before.

In the six years I spent in England and Ireland, I had forgotten about the generous hospitality in the Asian countries. My Moreira family whisked us away on a quick tour of Colombo, arriving back at their home for a luncheon repast of real Dutch Burgher food. The Sisters with me were overcome by the welcome, and some of the dishes were too hot for them; every dish was unique and to me quite wonderful as I had missed these flavours for the past six years. After the meal we caught up on family news and before we knew it, it was time to return to the ship before it set sail for Singapore. We thanked the family profusely and they took us back to the ship.

Our last stop would be Singapore. There we would begin our work in our recently completed custom built hospital. It would accommodate about two hundred patients in medical, surgical and maternity wings with operating theatres, labour wards and ancillary rooms. An area on the ground floor had been earmarked for physiotherapy treatments. The equipment for a physiotherapy department I had written back in England had been delivered, and was awaiting me; as Hospital Physiotherapist I looked forward to this as we drew closer to our destination.

We docked at Singapore and were met by two Sisters who had driven the hospital ambulance to meet us. Our luggage was stowed away in the back and we set forth in style to the new hospital. It was exciting to return to a bustling and beautiful island with so much to see. I had been away for six years.

We arrived at our 'hospital on the hill' called Mount Alvernia. Mount Alvernia is named in memory of the place where Saint Francis of Assisi had received his stigmata; the wounds Christ received when he was crucified. Many of our hospitals in different parts of the world have the same name for the same reasons; our Nursing Home in Guildford Surrey England, our hospital in Bulawayo in Africa, our hospital in Bendigo Australia, and now Mount Alvernia Singapore.

Catholic Properties

<u>*Malaysia:*</u>

- *Our Lady's Hospital, with Convent, Ipoh.*
- *Tan Tock Seng Hospital, Singapore, and Convent on the hospital grounds.*
- *Mount Alvernia Hospital, Singapore, Built 1960, by time Esmé returned to Singapore, Penthouse Chapel.*

<u>*United Kingdom:*</u>

- *Mount Alvernia Nursing Home, Guildford, Surrey with Penthouse Chapel.*
- *Portiuncula, Noviciate House, near Mount Alvernia Nursing Home, Guildford, Surrey.*
- *The Motherhouse, 'Ladywell', Convent with 100 acres in Godalming Surrey; where a new Chapel was being built.*
- *La Verna Nursing Home for Elders, Godalming Surrey, nuns slept in huts in the grounds.*
- *Portiuncula Hospital, Ballinasloe, Galway, Ireland, with Convent.*
- *Bishop's House, London. Convent where Esmé stayed during week while training as Physiotherapist, and at other times.*

11

Mount Alvernia Hospital

Mother Francis, Mother General and Foundress of the Franciscan Missionaries of the Divine Motherhood surveyed the community of Sisters at recreation at Mount Alvernia Hospital, Singapore. The year was 1960, and the custom built private hospital run and staffed by the Sisters, was to be officially opened by the Prime Minister, Mr Lee Kuan Yew.

'Sisters,' Mother Francis announced, 'we haven't much time. I've decided it would be interesting and unusual to have some paintings on the walls in the children's ward, one nursery rhyme scene above the eight beds. In the babies' ward, I have already painted a strip of sea above where the three new baby baths are placed. I would like many colourful fish painted on this ocean by referring to the National Geographic magazines provided. On the wide pillar between the milk kitchen and the premature baby unit, I intend painting the Boy Jesus. I need help to complete this before the opening in a five days time. Any volunteers?' Silence prevailed.

The Sisters knew the multi-talented Mother Foundress was gifted in many ways; artist, musician, writer, organizer, planner, you name it. Out of the nearly thirty Sisters, one voice piped up. Sister de Chantal was English, and said she would do her best and was willing to learn. I thought to myself, I'll give it a go.

'I'm good at drawing bones and joints, Mother. Is that any use?' I asked Mother Francis. Some of the Sisters giggled.

'Of course, Sister, I will be happy to teach you not just how to paint, but to flesh out your paintings so they jump out of the flat wall and look real. You'll be amazed. We'll start work tomorrow morning. Thank you everyone and good night, Sisters.'

The next morning after breakfast, we met in the empty children's ward. Mother Francis assigned us to the area above a bed and handed us picture books of nursery rhymes, oil paints, brushes, palettes, clothes, pencils and bowls of water. We wanted for nothing.

'To start with Sisters, go ahead and choose the scene and let me know so we don't have duplicates. With three of us doing this, there shouldn't be a problem.'

With that Mother sat to study her scene and Sister de Chantal and I did the same. After a quiet period, we collected our brushes, paints and ladders. The scene was on the wall behind each bed and above it, so ladders were necessary. I chose the *Old Woman who lived in the Shoe*, Sister de Chantal chose *Humpty Dumpty* and Mother Francis chose *Little Bo Peep*. There were eight beds in this ward, so there were five more scenes to do after we finished the first three.

I stood back, sized up the wall and made a light border for the scene to fit in above the bed-head. Opening the book at the page with the picture, I mounted the ladder and sketched the outline of the picture. Before I started to fill in with paint, Mother Francis came over.

'Good work Sister, now this here and over there needs to be smaller and bigger respectively, and remember the proportions of the children compared to the size of the shoe. Start with the basic colour and gradually paint over till you get the desired effect.'

Mother Francis inspected Sister de Chantal's work and made helpful suggestions. After working silently for a while, we began to see *Humpty Dumpty*, *Bo Peep* and the *Old Woman in the Shoe* emerge.

The odor of oil paints filled the air, but was tolerable. Hours later the pictures were almost complete. At this stage, Mother Francis asked us to choose the next story we intended to illustrate. The scenes we chose were *Jack Spratt*, the *Lion and the Unicorn* and *Wee Willie Winkie*. Sister de Chantal and I found that the person we thought would be intimidating to work with, was actually helpful, appreciative of our efforts and encouraging. We finished our paintings and chose the last two scenes; *The Man in the Moon* and *The Robin and the Squirrel*.

The next morning we got to work and Mother Francis finished off her second picture. Evening was approaching as we put the finishing touches to our second work, that was until Mother Francis checked each picture carefully and asked us to make changes. An hour later we had incorporated her suggestions, and left for our evening ritual.

The following morning, Mother Francis stood at the base of each bed in turn, intently studying the scene above the head of the bed. We adjusted a few details according to her advice on each painting.
'I'm very pleased with your efforts Sisters. You have made great strides in your work, the colours are lively, the scene tells the story and because of our different styles, there is variety in the whole room. It should keep the children amused and interested, trying to figure out the story in each scene. Good work and

congratulations. Tomorrow we will work in the newly born nursery.'

The next day, Mother Francis gave us some National Geographical magazines saying that we should choose any fish that lived in the deep oceans and paint them onto the sea. It was fun to choose from the many exotic fish of different shapes and colours we saw in those magazines. We set to work and Mother Francis worked alongside us pausing at times to oversee what we had painted and advising where necessary. Before long we could see a colourful border of fish swimming in the deep ocean, above the baby baths.

Mother Francis moved to the central pillar that separated the milk kitchen from the premature unit. She called me to her side.
'Sister, I am going to paint the Boy Jesus in the Hummel tradition in the middle, but I want you to paint birds around the Boy Jesus. You will find different types of birds in this National Geographic magazine. Go ahead and paint as many different ones as you can, making them as lifelike as possible.' Having finished with the fish in the ocean, I moved to where Mother Francis was working on the Boy Jesus. Placing my stool in the doorway of the Premie Unit as we called it, I started with birds on one side of Boy Jesus that Mother Francis was working on. The numerous types of birds made my choices easy and soon I had finished one side. But time was over for the day and tomorrow was the opening.

More birds chosen from the National Geographic photos took shape on the other side of Boy Jesus. Time was against us as we had just two hours until the Opening Ceremony. Mother Francis and I worked hard. Finally we stood back to see the work as a whole.

'Good work, Sisters. If changes are necessary we can do them afterwards. We have a short time to get ourselves cleaned up and ready for the opening of the hospital. Thank you for your work over the week and I have to say I am proud of you for stepping up. Now just clear up the paints and tools and let's get ready for the opening.' We quickly showered and dressed for the Grand Opening.

I felt honored that in the short time working with her, that she trusted me to work beside her. That was uplifting for me.

Years later I heard that the hospital had further expanded and the paintings in the children's eight bed ward and the babies' nursery had been painted over. The rooms changed function. It seems sad to me.

* * * * *

The Feast of Saint Francis of Assisi, the most important feast day in the Franciscan calendar was on October 4, 1961. That year we were privileged to have with us the Foundress of our order. Celebrations at Vespers would be solemnly sung instead of the customary chanting. Mother Francis had flown from England with her companion Mother Immaculata, to be present for the opening of the first private hospital in Singapore, staffed and run by Franciscan nuns.

Mount Alvernia Hospital was built from donations; from the generous public in Singapore and partly by the donation from the Government. The Prime Minister of Singapore, the Honorable Lee Kuan Yew, had promised the Sisters that the government would match whatever the Sisters collected dollar for dollar.

The community assembled outside the Chapel entrance; Professed Sisters donned their sky blue veils over their white everyday veils, before entering the Chapel to worship. I had agreed to play our small harmonium which was controlled by the feet pumping the bellows. Several of the Sisters were much more experienced organists but refused to play because Mother General herself excelled at playing a keyboard, and they were afraid of not measuring up to her standards. As for me, I knew I could barely scrape by as an organist, but the difference was that I was not afraid of Mother General.

So, here I was, playing softly a solemn piece of music, as the Sisters entered the Chapel. They took their places in the carved seats of oak, positioned along the side walls, and at the back of the Chapel were three seats with kneelers; the Mother General was in the centre, her companion on her left, and the local Superior on her right. I was seated at the organ in line with them, also facing the altar.

Two chantresses stood at the lectern on which rested the large volume of the psalms. Singing the first line of the first verse of the Feast, the first Chantress started Vespers. I played the accompaniment and the community joined in, each side singing alternate verses.

Gregorian Chant is one of the most difficult of choral music pieces to sing, and it is one of the most beautiful. Many pieces of lighter music begin with harmonies taken from the Gregorian Chant. I loved singing it; whenever we sang it at the important festivals I could imagine soaring into the heavens on the wings of these melodies.

The hospital was new and everything in it, including the furniture which was custom built by a contractor. It so happened, that one batch of stools supplied had a flaw. This had been discovered in the patients' rooms and throughout the hospital.

Never dreaming that the stool I sat on at the organ was one of these, I was happily playing when suddenly an almighty crack sounded. I glanced around quickly and then before I knew it, the stool broke in half and I was sitting on the floor, feet in the air.

After the initial shock, I jumped up and standing on one foot I frantically started pumping the organ bellows with the other foot to carry on with the playing, thinking to myself, the show must go on. Then I realised that no one was singing. The Sisters and the senior Reverend Mothers in line with the organ were doing their best to control their laughter; they were purple in the face from this exertion.

One of the Sisters found another stool and kindly brought it to me. Again the music flowed and the Sisters started to sing once more. We completed Vespers and everyone filed out of the Chapel.

However, it was not until we met again later at recreation that we could talk about this hilarious event. We recalled the Chapel one moment awash in solemn song and a moment later the loud crack, and the recreation room was filled with laughter at the memory of my butt crashing to the floor.

* * * * *

We planned to sing the Mass of Saint Cecilia who was the Patron Saint of Musicians, for midnight Mass on

Christmas Eve 1963. Many weeks of practice had prepared us for the event.

I loved the opportunity of being Choir Mistress at this time. It meant I could tell the Mother Superior how I wanted it sung, as she was in the choir, along with the other Sisters, many were senior to me in religious life. It was great fun and I relished every moment of my short lived glory.

Our Mass was held in the penthouse Chapel at Mount Alvernia Hospital in Singapore. It was a beautiful Chapel with a spotlessly clean and shiny parquet floor, brand new of course, pews for about fifteen nuns along the length of the Chapel, facing one another. The choir was positioned at the back of the Chapel, near the organ. A few patients and visitors sat in the pews normally occupied by the Sisters.

Sisters who were not on duty in the hospital were dressed in sky blue veils and gathered with lungs pumped to do justice to the beautiful harmonies of the Mass of Saint Cecilia.

Intoning the first lines of the Kyrie in Latin, I silently gave thanks for the chance to lead the choir in singing this age-old Mass. After Vatican II Pope John XXIII had announced Masses could be performed in the language of the country, whereas previously, only Latin was acceptable. The Mass of Saint Cecilia was not widely sung, but it was much appreciated by aficionados of sung Latin Masses.

The Gloria followed with the uplifting strains of its own praises, and the Sisters continued to sing in fine voice, harmonies included. The homily followed the Readings and then the Offertory was sung in a quieter tone as we approached the solemn part of the Mass; the Consecration of the Bread and Wine.

A hush settled over the gathering as we prepared to sing the Sanctus. Just as I raised my hand to start, a rather large and seemingly lost cockroach crossed between the choir and me, appearing to be aimed for the other side of the Chapel. He meandered nonchalantly along unaware of the horror he was creating by his mere presence. How could this happen on such a spotlessly clean parquet floor that almost reflected the Sisters in its shine. For a moment I was in a quandary; then I decided this was probably not the right time to execute this insect.

Once the giggles had died down I gave the sign to start singing. The reverence, with which the Sanctus was sung, was remarkable considering the giggles that went before. Meanwhile, the cockroach had disappeared from view and we were back in action. The divinely elegant music floated through the Chapel as we approached Communion and the memory of the cockroach's sojourn was forgotten.

All in all, the Mass of Saint Cecilia inspired us to the climax of welcoming the arrival of the Infant Child into our world that warm Singapore night, despite the efforts of the cockroach to distract us.

Postscript:

The exterminators were busy in the Chapel the next day.

Mt Alvernia Hospital in Singapore has continued to flourish.
https://en.wikipedia.org/wiki/Mount_Alvernia_Hospital

Sister Regina Mundi after Final Vows
Singapore 6th January 1961
From Esmé's Photograph Album

12

Good Judgment

Five nuns of the Franciscan Missionaries of the Divine Motherhood had squeezed into the little 1961 Morris car. Mother Francis trusted my driving so had asked me to do the driving as I knew the roads and my way around the different cities. At the end of a two day visit to Ipoh we went to early Mass followed by a good breakfast provided by our kind hostesses, the Dames de Saint Maur Sisters. Our hostesses belonged to a group of Missionaries who ran excellent schools in Malaysia and Singapore. I had been taught by them as a child, so it was a happy reunion for me. We thanked them for their hospitality and left.

The three other Sisters in our car were Superiors, traveling with Mother Francis who was the Mother General and Foundress of this group of Franciscan nuns. Mother Francis had flown to Singapore from England, accompanied by two of her Council Members, Mother Immaculata and Mother Benedict. The fourth nun was Mother Angela, who was in charge of Mount Alvernia Hospital in Singapore and Regional Superior for our hospice in Penang, Malaysia. I was the youngest and the only ordinary Sister amongst these high ranking Superiors.

The journey to Singapore from Ipoh was a mere 450 miles of travel through countryside varying in vegetation from acres of rice fields to plantations of rubber and palm oil, interspersed with thick jungle in the uninhabited areas. Inland temperatures in the tropics range from 70°F-90°F or 21°C–33°C, with humidity registering between 90%-95%. Malaysia and Singapore are just five degrees north of the Equator, so days can be very warm indeed.

It was customary for FMDM nuns when traveling in a car, for everyone to recite in unison a prayer called *The Memorare*, for a safe journey. This time our prayer was heard. Deftly, I navigated the little car over the familiar roads, fully aware of the responsibility of transporting these important women. From Ipoh to Kuala Lumpur it normally took three hours in ordinary traffic. About thirty miles outside Kuala Lumpur were many lengthy S-bends through the winding mountain roads, which meant overtaking was virtually impossible for many miles.

Mother Francis was seated in the front beside me and the other Mothers chatted amiably in the back seat, whilst Mother Immaculata passed a bag of sweets around.

Approaching an S-bend, I noticed a long double trailer lorry, wider than usual, ahead of us. Conscious of the location, the curves of the road and the danger of overtaking, I kept my distance behind it. A few moments passed when to my surprise, waving her hand imperiously, Mother Francis commanded, 'Pass him, Sister!'

Remembering my Vow of Obedience, but against my better judgment, I sized up the situation, took a deep breath and moved the car into the oncoming lane.

Nothing appeared to be approaching us, so I accelerated and our car moved alongside the trailer.

It seemed to take ages, as it was a long vehicle and was moving much faster than such vehicles' speed limits are permitted. Just as I drew abreast, ahead I saw a huge trailer of similar length loom into view. It was rapidly bearing down on us. Mind and reflexes racing, I stepped harder on the accelerator and we shot forward. But it was not fast enough to overtake the lorry. The approaching vehicle rapidly drew abreast with the lorry on our left and we were squeezed in between. We were the meat in the sandwich.

Time stood still; a hair's breadth separated the three moving vehicles. We all held our breaths! In the next moment we were free; miraculously unscathed, and the trucks were behind us. Looking in my rear mirror, I could see their size diminishing, as we forged ahead.

Mother Francis kept silent but with a quick glance I saw her face looked pale. I wondered what she was thinking as I drove on, stoically concentrating on the road ahead. The atmosphere in the car was electric. From the back seat, Mother Benedict inhaled loudly and giggled.

'I had such a fright just now, I swallowed my sweet!'

* * * * *

At a later date, Sister Mercy and I were assigned to visit Ipoh to raise funds and collect donations to further our missionary and hospital work in Ipoh and Singapore, and later in Penang. We stayed overnight at the local Convent. During this time we visited my family home and I was able to have precious time with my parents and my mother's German Shepherd dog, Rex.

Sister Regina Mundi 1962
At home, Ipoh Malaysia, collecting donations
for FMDM hospital.
From Esmé's Photograph Album

13

Final Decisions

July 6 1961 dawned on a warm Singapore morning and as I woke I was excited in anticipation of what would happen in a few hours time. It was the day I made my Final Vows of my Profession as a Franciscan Nun. I was the only Novice making my Final Vows and the first one to do so in the new Chapel at Mount Alvernia, Singapore.

There had been many ups and downs over the last seven and a half years. At times I was near to wanting out and at other times I was happy. At that particular time I felt the calling to dedicate my life to the rule and life of the Sisters. I had been truly tested and the next step was a valid one; making the Final Commitment.

During the ceremony in the Chapel, I bowed to this commitment by prostrating myself on the floor in front of the officiating priest who read the appropriate prayers for the occasion. I was questioned and I answered. I stood to receive the ring on my right ring finger to seal the marriage to Christ, and lastly a Crown of Thorns in recognition of the Crown of Thorns worn by Jesus at the time of His crucifixion was placed on my head and it remained on until I retired.

My mother flew to Singapore from Ipoh for the occasion and after the ceremony and celebrations we were able to spend time together. All in all it was a day to remember.

* * * * *

I sat waiting in the dimly lit foyer of the Singapore hospital at the late hour of 9:30 pm for my mother and sister to pick me up. The hospital was quiet for the night, the Sisters in bed and I sat waiting, wearing strange clothing, apparently alone except for the reduced activity in the general medical wards. I anxiously watched the pitch black night outside, waiting to see car's lights climb the hill toward the hospital. The silence of Mount Alvernia Hospital that night contrasted starkly to the busy scene during the day.

In the silence of the empty foyer, the thrill of impending freedom coursed through my being; knowing that I was about to leave the last ten years of my life as a Franciscan nun behind. I would be free to make my own choices in my life, in the big bad world. The hairs stood up on my arms and legs, and shivers ran through my body as I remembered the decade. There had been times when I felt truly happy, but times when I longed to get away, to live my life without the many constraints that were a necessary part of being a nun. I knew now that a religious life was not for me, and waves of relief flowed through me, knowing I would presently be back with my loving family and I would be free to choose another path in my life.

Bright lights spliced the dark night as a car drew near the hospital entrance and parked. Standing up, I could see my sister was driving and my mother seated next to her. Emerging from a side corridor, the Mother Superior hurried forward to greet my family at the door. Obviously she too had been watching from her office for their arrival. Greetings over, she wished me a happy future life with many blessings and saying goodbye to us all, she waved us on our way. Short and sweet.

I hugged my mother and sister. I had mixed emotions as I settled in the back seat; I felt happiness to be totally free and sadness at leaving the many friends I had made amongst the Sisters.

We drove to a nearby motel where we spent the night, before leaving early the next morning on the eight hour drive from Singapore to Ipoh, our home town in Northern Malaysia. There would be time for talking on that journey, as I'm sure my mother and sister had many questions. I thanked them for their support and for making the long journey to Singapore, to pick me up.

I had spent the day rushing around the hospital, discharging my various duties as Hospital Physiotherapist, Admissions Sister, and helper on the maternity floor. These responsibilities would be divided amongst the remaining Sisters. I wanted to be sure that all was left in order.

Months earlier I had written to the Mother General in England, who founded this congregation, asking for a dispensation from the Vows of Poverty, Chastity and Obedience. She replied asking if I was completely sure, and if I was, to sign the enclosed letter to the Pope and post it to Rome direct.

Before the Second Vatican Council dispensation from Vows was rare. If a nun wanted to leave, she had to write to the Pope, as our group of Sisters were a Papal Congregation so 'big decisions' had to be made alongside the Pope. Now after Vatican 11, Nuns can be absolved from their Vows by their own Superior. These changes make things easier for those wishing to leave the convent or seminary.

Three months later the reply arrived. Mother Angela, the Sister Superior of Singapore, called me to her room and informed me that she had arranged for my mother and sister to pick me up at 9:30 pm that evening, when the Sisters had retired to their quarters. I was forbidden to tell any of the Sisters that I was leaving. Mother gave me a suitcase of clothing and other personal items, which was to be stored in a cupboard, out of sight, until the time came to make the change from nun to ordinary citizen.

She advised me that an announcement about my departure would be made the following day. From that day on no one would be allowed to refer to me in any way and I was not to try to communicate with any of the Sisters either. I heard later that when the announcement of my departure was made to the community, many of the Sisters were shocked and several Sisters burst into tears.

For my part, as we drove back to Ipoh from Singapore we enjoyed chatting again. Ten years had passed and we had to get to know one another again. It was a great reunion especially when we arrived home; my father rushed out to greet us with open arms. We were together again; a happy family.

I left on Thursday 24 September 1964. I was now thirty one years of age. My parents were happy so perhaps my decade as a nun had healed their differences. I certainly have had an eventful enjoyable life from that day onwards. I am proud to say I was once a nun.

Esmé's Favourite Psalm

[1] It is good to give thanks

to the LORD
And to sing praises to Your name,
O Most High;
[2] To declare Your loving kindness
in the morning,
And Your faithfulness every night,
[3] On an instrument of ten strings,
On the lute,
And on the harp,
With harmonious sound.
[4] For You, LORD, have made me glad
through Your work;

Franciscan Tau Cross

St Francis of Assisi   *Saint Clare & Saint Francis*

14

More Follow

Many weeks later, I received an unexpected letter. It was from one of the Sisters who had promised to keep in touch, albeit illegally. Sister Vonna told me that she and another Sister found life in the FMDM community intolerable, and were seriously contemplating leaving. This surprised me as I had no idea they had been unhappy when I left. Aware of what life was like I offered to help them in the future if they needed it. In her letter Sister Vonna said they had come to the end of their individual ropes. To prepare for the day, when patients on their maternity floor donated money to them, as Sisters in Charge of maternity floor, Sister Vonna put the money in a box. In order to get letters posted and to receive replies, they took one of their lay nurses into their confidence. Letters flew back and forth and with each one, more and more details of their disenchantment with religious life were revealed. At the end of each letter Sister Vonna asked that I destroy her letters to avoid any repercussions.

As time passed I read more desperation in the tone of her letters. Each time I replied my advice was to do it the approved way, as I had done, and to apply for dispensation from their Vows through the customary channels; the Pope. But they were adamant; they were going to walk out and disappear.

One evening as our family watched the television news the phone rang. I was dumbfounded to hear Sister Vonna say, 'Esmé, we are out! We're staying with a friend who offered to house us until we sort ourselves out.'
'Did you get your dispensation?'
'No, we decided we'd had enough, so we set ourselves up with the necessities and after the Sisters had gone to bed, we stayed on in the hospital building, changed our clothes, called a taxi, and here we are!'
'Wow! You are brave to do it this way. Do you think they will find you?' I asked in awe of their actions.
'I doubt it,' came the quick reply. 'They are too busy with the visit of Mother General from England. This helped us make our minds up, and seize the opportunity to make a quick get-away!'
'Are you able to fly to Ipoh and spend some time with me and we can catch up? Firstly, have you got enough funds for your air fares?'
'Oh yes! Our patients donated enough for us to go a long way. They were so generous.'

Thoughts flew through my mind; here were two nuns, older than me, both had been in religious life much longer than me, and they too wanted to be free of the shackles of Franciscan life. They were certified Nurses and Midwives and highly thought of in their careers by the senior nuns in their community and by the doctors and nurses they worked with.

The difficulty was they had no support from their families, whereas I did. Vonna was Singaporean Chinese, whose family had been totally opposed to her becoming a nun. Maggie was British and had no family to help her. The friend who kindly offered them refuge in Singapore was a well known obstetrician and
100

gynaecologist with whom they had worked from the time Mount Alvernia Hospital opened.

Returning to our conversation, I suggested, 'Make your arrangements to fly from Singapore to Ipoh, and leave your return flight open. You are welcome to stay with us as long as you like. We can talk things over, and no doubt my Dad will be able to advise you too.'

Vonna spoke to Maggie at the other end and came back to our conversation. 'We're so looking forward to seeing you and having a good talk and thank you so much for having us. We'll let you know our arrival details when we have them confirmed.'

'It'll be great to see you again and we'll have lots of fun. Hopefully, I can get some leave from my job, and we'll have lots of time to talk and talk, remembering we've kept the Rule of Silence for so many years! Talk soon, bye for now.'

A few days later on my lunch break at home I was told by my sister who had a day off that the Reverend Mother and another Sister from the local FMDM hospital in Ipoh, Our Lady's Hospital, had arrived at our home unexpectedly and asked if the two Sisters from Singapore were staying with us. Thankfully my sister had the presence of mind to play dumb; she didn't know who and what they were talking about. This, however, was a warning that the nuns in Ipoh had been advised by their Singapore Sisters about two nuns leaving of their own accord and their whereabouts was a mystery. Apparently, they knew of our friendship and suspected that the two Sisters had turned to me for help!

Three days later I was at my local airport in Ipoh waiting for their arrival from Singapore. The Fokker Friendship Malaysian Airlines plane arrived on time

and I watched as they descended the steps from the plane. Being a domestic flight there were no formalities, so I was able to meet them directly at the arrival gate. Warm greetings and hugs were exchanged and I asked if they had more luggage to collect.
'Everything we have is here with us.'

My mother welcomed them into our home and I showed them their room. We returned to the lounge and sat down to talk. I offered them a cold drink which they gratefully accepted, and we launched into an animated question and answer session on their story.
'Let's start at the beginning and I'll replenish your glasses with gin, as you go on.' We laughed at this, and the story began.

Life had grown more and more intolerable for Maggie and Vonna as Sisters in Charge of the Maternity floor at night and during the day; due to the constant negative criticism and witch-hunt that went on and on. This wore them down and they decided to follow my example and leave religious life. They could no longer tolerate their treatment and the unfairness of the judgments by the hospital hierarchy. They decided not to wait. One of their nurses got the basic items to change out of habit into lay clothes and other immediate necessities. Generous donations from patients paid for these items along with a medium sized suitcase each, with a handbag. Singapore was and is a haven for shopping. The Sisters decided to stick together and were relieved that a long time colleague understood their situation. When they had the items they required, the date for 'The Exit' was set, and it was to be soon.

When the night arrived, they remained on duty which was not unusual for the maternity floor. The Sisters and Superior retired and Maggie and Vonna changed into their mufti clothes, picked up the belongings they
102

needed, left their nuns' clothing in a corner of the bathroom and hurried out to the nurse's station. Sending one of the lay nurses to check that the coast was clear they phoned for a taxi and off they went with only their trusted nurse to see them leave.

Next morning, it was not until breakfast that the absence of the two nuns was noticed. Reverend Mother was alerted and the hospital searched. When the nurses on the maternity floor were questioned and seemed to know nothing, Reverend Mother feared the worst; they had absconded. Two Sisters had vanished without a trace. Trusted nurses proved untrustworthy.

Meanwhile the first person suspected to have helped the Sisters was none other than me! I told Maggie and Vonna how the local Reverend Mother had arrived at our front doorstep asking for them, and of my sister's reply; that she neither knew the Sisters nor their whereabouts.

When the two women returned to Singapore they were met by nuns at the Airport and they were taken back to the convent. Singaporean Vonna was transferred to England and later to Africa from where she decided to leave via the proper channels. British Maggie returned to religious life and decided to stay, and is still in service to God to this day.

Mother Superior wrongly accused me of aiding and abetting their departure. My conscience was clear as I had repeatedly encouraged them to ask for dispensation, and leave in good grace.

The End

Acknowledgements

Names have been changed where necessary to protect my sisters who are, or maybe still in service to God.

Photographs printed in this book are from the private collection of Esmé Moreira, apart from photographs which come from the internet websites.

I would like to thank Sue Shabazz for the initial proof reading, Barbara Taylor of Christchurch, New Zealand for the thorough editing, Kimberly Kinser for the Beta Read, and everyone else who encouraged and begged me to finish this book.

And special thanks to Julie my wife, who has cared for me and given me the love I've been looking for all my life.

Summary of Esmé's Life as a Nun
of the order of the
Franciscan Missionaries of the Divine Motherhood

06.01.54	Entered as a **Postulant**, in Singapore for 2 months, then transferred to England on 6.3.54.	Aged 20 years
06.03.54	Trained for 6 months as a 'Blue Apron'	
7.54	After six months: **Ceremony of Clothing,** named **Sister Regina Mundi.** Now a **Novice**	
7.56	**Novice,** for two years then deemed suitable to take **First Vows,** or make one's **First Profession.** Known as **Blue Veil, YBV** or **Professed Sister.**	
9.56	Started Physiotherapy Training London	2 ½ years (18 months)
12.59	Return to Singapore after 5 years, renewed Vows each year	
06.07.61	At the 5th renewal took her **Final Vows,** Ring on right hand.	7 years
04.10.61	Mount Alvernia Hospital officially opened in Singapore	7 ½ years
24.09.64	Esmé left Religious Life	10 years Aged 31 years

12951993R00066

Made in the USA
San Bernardino, CA
12 December 2018